Suck Less in the Classroom Tomorrow

Suck Less in the Classroom Tomorrow is an honest and comprehensive guide for struggling classroom teachers looking to improve their craft. Part narrative, part guidebook, it offers an overview of the profession, with practical advice, easy-to-implement strategies, and how-to information for the day-to-day of teaching, written as a conversation overheard in the teachers' lounge.

Unlike traditional teacher guides, this book calls it like it is and says the quiet parts out loud. It helps struggling teachers feel seen and know that not everyone has it all figured out all the time. The easy-to-digest chapters cover sucking less at lesson planning, classroom management, grading and feedback, burning out, and more. An appendix offers a list of "plug-and-chug" strategies that a teacher can start using on day one—what they are, how to use them, and ways they can show up in your classroom.

With the helpful and humorous advice in this book, you'll feel inspired to teach better while also being reassured that teaching is hard and we don't have to be perfect every day. Little by little, you will improve and find your joy and satisfaction increasing along the way.

Carlton Glassford has been in education for nearly two decades. He has been a classroom teacher, an instructional coach, and a district-level administrator. He has observed hundreds of hours of classroom instruction and knows what works, but more importantly, what doesn't work in the classroom. In 2014, he was named the "Outstanding Educator of the Year" for his school. He has developed his craft in Indiana, the Bronx, New York, San Jose, California, and now outside Portland, Oregon. He is ardently focused on improving at teaching and helping others improve as well.

Suck Less in the Classroom Tomorrow

Honest Advice for Teachers in their First Years

Carlton Glassford

Routledge
Taylor & Francis Group
NEW YORK AND LONDON

Designed cover image: Getty Images

First published 2026
by Routledge
605 Third Avenue, New York, NY 10158

and by Routledge
4 Park Square, Milton Park, Abingdon, Oxon, OX14 4RN

Routledge is an imprint of the Taylor & Francis Group, an informa business

© 2026 Carlton Glassford

The right of Carlton Glassford to be identified as author of this work has been asserted in accordance with sections 77 and 78 of the Copyright, Designs and Patents Act 1988.

All rights reserved. No part of this book may be reprinted or reproduced or utilised in any form or by any electronic, mechanical, or other means, now known or hereafter invented, including photocopying and recording, or in any information storage or retrieval system, without permission in writing from the publishers.

For Product Safety Concerns and Information please contact our EU representative GPSR@taylorandfrancis.com. Taylor & Francis Verlag GmbH, Kaufingerstraße 24, 80331 München, Germany.

Trademark notice: Product or corporate names may be trademarks or registered trademarks, and are used only for identification and explanation without intent to infringe.

ISBN: 978-1-041-19694-5 (hbk)
ISBN: 978-1-041-19692-1 (pbk)
ISBN: 978-1-003-71289-3 (ebk)

DOI: 10.4324/9781003712893

Typeset in Palatino
by codeMantra

For Megan, thank you for always believing in and supporting me. I couldn't have done this without you.
For Finneas, thank you for giving me the best teaching job I could ever ask for.
Lastly, to all my students, past, present, and future, thank you for trusting me and helping me grow.

Contents

Acknowledgments..viii
About the Author..ix

1. Why Suck Less: Progress over Perfection 1

2. Suck Less at Lesson Planning: From Objectives to
   Exit Ticket and Everything in Between 6

3. Suck Less at Classroom Management: Control
   What You Can, Ignore What You Can't..................45

4. Suck Less at Grading and Feedback: Tips and
   Tricks to Make Grading Sustainable 78

5. Suck Less at Burnout: How to Stay Up When
   You're Under Water 94

6. Suck Less Together: Building Community and
   Support Structures That Last 112

7. Suck Less at Getting Better: Self-Improvement
   Strategies for a Busy Teacher 124

8. Suck Less at Everything Else: Lessons I Wish I'd
   Known When I Started 135

   Epilogue: Suck Less Tomorrow: How It Started,
   How It's Going 142

   Appendix: Field-Tested Strategies 147

Acknowledgments

First, thank you to my family. My wife Megan who has never stopped believing in me and encourages me to take risks. My mother for cheering me on and my parents-in-law for the hours of time they provided for me to see this project through.

I am deeply grateful to my editor, Lauren Davis, and Hannah Sroka at Taylor & Francis, for their guidance, care, and for taking a chance on this project, helping to shape it into the book it has become.

I would not be the teacher I am today without the school leaders who guided me, trusted me, and gave me opportunities to grow

To my Wildcat family, thank you for pushing me, challenging me, and helping me grow as an educator, with a special thank you to Nathan Foor for his mentorship and feedback.

A special thank you to Josh Craig for always being a phone call away and spending countless hours talking teaching with me over the years.

A big thank you, Billie, for your thoughtful contributions and feedback.

To my friends and colleagues who read early drafts, offered feedback, and encouraged me to keep going—Colin, Heather, Michelle, Julie, Jeremiah, Justin, and Lydia, thank you for everything.

Special thanks to Emily M. for her creative input.

Finally, thank you to anyone who has, in some way, contributed to this work, whether it was through conversation, encouragement, or simply believing that this book could be written.

About the Author

Carlton Glassford has been a passionate educator since 2008—and a proficient one since about 2012. He's taught in classrooms across Indiana, New York, California, and now Oregon, primarily serving Title I schools and diverse student communities. Carlton currently teaches high school Civics, Economics, AVID, and Personal Finance.

Over the years, he has taught just about every social studies class there is, coached new teachers, presented at national conferences, spent time as a district-level administrator, and served as a CASA volunteer, advocating for children in the foster care system. Through it all, one belief has stuck with him: teachers don't have to be perfect to make a meaningful impact.

Stemming from his work with struggling teachers, Carlton adopted the philosophy that perfection doesn't need to be the goal but that if you can just "suck less tomorrow" then you're already doing something right. And that mantra is what inspired him to write this book.

When not teaching, you will likely find Carlton running his school's Dungeons & Dragons Club, out for a hike, cooking plant-based meals, or playing Settlers of Catan. He resides in Oregon with his loving wife Megan, their amazing son Finneas, and their dog Parker, who would be perfect if he didn't shed so much.

1

Why Suck Less: Progress over Perfection

Why not "Be Great"? Or "Transform into a Super Teacher"? Because some days, in teaching, all you can hope for is to suck a little less tomorrow than you did today. Teaching is a difficult profession. I once knew a teacher who cried every single day of the school year. Every. Single. Day. A teacher in that situation doesn't need to hear "Be great!" or "Teach like a champion!" What that teacher needs to hear is that change is possible. The goal is not total transformation—the goal is improvement.

> Change is possible. The goal is not total transformation—the goal is improvement.

There are a ton of books out there that aim to transform a person into a "great" teacher. Trust me, I've read most of them. When we wrap this profession in the language of "champions" and "greatness," we set ourselves up against standards that feel unreachable, especially when we're just trying to survive the day. The last thing anyone needs is a book that makes them feel like a failure for not being fantastic in the classroom.

This book won't grant you teaching super-powers, but it will help you make it through the week. It will give you the practical tools you need to improve, without a million steps to complete or a new acronym to memorize. Think of it as a manual for getting a little bit better, one day at a time.

Getting a Little Better Each Day

I believe in the necessity of self-improvement for educators. I believe teachers should aim for continuous growth in their profession and that they should make use of every resource available to that end. If I didn't believe that, I wouldn't be writing this book. I'd be rehashing the same lesson each year and passing out worksheets as they grow on trees.

Here's the truth: you might struggle with teaching. I still come up short at times myself. Teaching is hard. Like, really hard. We're wearing a million different hats, juggling the needs of 35 children, and trying to hit our learning goals. We all need a little extra help now and again. The good news, though? Teachers have been doing this for centuries, and we don't have to do it all in a vacuum or reinvent the wheel each year.

Why This Book?

There are some great teaching books out there. But comprehensive guides to reaching classroom nirvana can be overwhelming when you're first starting. Sometimes schools, professional development, and books send a lot our way while we're still trying to figure out how to take attendance.

Think of this book as an analogue to that teacher in the lounge who has *seen some stuff*. This book is nearly two decades of hard-earned classroom lessons, distilled into something that fits in your bag or desk drawer, wherever you need it most. In the following pages, I'll be discussing my approaches to lesson planning, classroom management, and the day-to-day tasks of the profession. This book won't do it all. But it will help you do something, and sometimes, that's enough.

Why Me?

Why do I feel qualified to write this book? Because I've learned how to be a better teacher the hard way. It took me years to figure out my moves, and then additional years to refine them.

My first-year teaching was a total disaster. I was teaching eighth grade, had zero experience with middle schoolers, and possessed absolutely no plan. I yelled constantly, made some truly ridiculous attempts to gain control, and upon conclusion of the school year, I wasn't asked back.

My second job didn't go much better. I was hired in October by a tiny, brand-new charter school. I thought I was getting the hang of being a teacher, but by winter break, I was asked to resign. Another misstep on my way to becoming the teacher I am today.

After that, I left teaching for a few months. And those were a sad few months of my life. I wasn't in a classroom, the place I knew I needed to be and wanted to be. So, I moved back home and started substitute teaching, all while working on improving my craft. It was the best decision of my life.

Subbing *is* classroom management. I had to figure it out or get eaten alive. I read a couple of teaching books and practiced their strategies daily with new students. The beauty of subbing is that if you screw up with one class and they get a little out of control, you get a do-over the next day. It's rinse and repeat for your teacher moves. And it was substitute teaching that helped me land my next teaching job.

The principal at the school I subbed at had heard great things about me and hired me on the spot the next year based on my reputation alone. I finally found my footing in a high school. I excelled at that position; that isn't to say I didn't struggle at times. But during this time, I was promoted to the role of Mentor Teacher, where I coached teachers and evaluated teachers while maintaining my regular classroom duties. A further promotion to Master Teacher followed that. (A Master Teacher is what most schools would call an instructional coach.) This role took me out of the classroom, and I had to evaluate half the teachers in my building, lead weekly professional development seminars, and coach about a quarter of the teachers at my school. During my time as Master Teacher, I was able to observe hundreds of classroom interactions and lessons. This experience made me acutely aware that many of us are experiencing the same issues in the classroom.

I eventually left the role of Master Teacher to go back into the classroom. A year later, I moved to New York City and brought my teacher to a charter school in the Bronx. I was quickly recognized in New York as a strong teacher and was promoted to support new teachers.

I had gotten my master's in school leadership and left New York to try my hand as a district-level administrator for a charter network in Gary, Indiana. This position led me to support classrooms and evaluate teachers from kindergarten all the way up to post-high school.

I've seen the gamut of classrooms and have witnessed what works and doesn't work across the board. I've tried the strategies in this book across the country: at two Title I (federally funded schools serving mostly low-income students) schools in Northwest Indiana, a Title I charter school in the Bronx, New York, at another Title I school in East San Jose, and at an affluent school just outside Portland, Oregon. These approaches work. They've worked for me in schools with all kinds of students, and they can work for you, too, if you're willing to put in the practice. I'm here to tell you you're not alone. Things *can* get better.

How to Use This Book

Like most books of this nature, you don't have to read it cover to cover. Start with the topics that feel most urgent, or you can read it straight through if that fits your fancy.

The architecture of this book is essentially divided into two parts. The first part of this book begins with lesson planning and classroom management, because that is the nuts and bolts of the profession. The second part of this book continues into grading, work-life balance, and interpersonal relationships at work. I've learned a lot there as well.

It doesn't matter how you came to this profession or why you're here; at the end of the day, what matters is that you haven't given up yet. However, you use this book—skimming for survival or reading it on a weekend—I hope it gives you something: a winning strategy. A reason to laugh. Or perhaps a reminder that we all struggle sometimes, and if we take the time to learn from those struggles, we can all suck a little less tomorrow.

2

Suck Less at Lesson Planning: From Objectives to Exit Ticket and Everything in Between

If you've ever run out of material mid-lesson and had to ask yourself, "Now what?" You know the importance of lesson planning.

Lesson planning can often be the difference between a good day and chaos. In theory, it's simple. Think about what you want students to learn and then what steps you'll take to get them there. In practice, though, it can be incredibly difficult.

In college or your teacher prep program, you likely made lesson plans that were long and detailed. They were beasts packed with multi-tiered learning objectives, visuals for every slide, differentiation strategies, closure activities, and even extension plans if you ran out of time.

Here's the truth that they don't tell you in college: you do not have time to plan like that every day.

And more importantly, you don't need to.

Thanksgiving Dinner

A really well-planned lesson is like Thanksgiving dinner. You've got your main dish, a dozen sides, a perfectly set table, and a dessert you'd post to your Instagram. However, the kitchen looks like a war zone, and you need a nap. Sure, it's beautiful, but you're exhausted, and it's totally unsustainable.

That's why we don't cook Thanksgiving every night. It's just not practical, and it's not necessary.

That isn't to say you won't still cook some incredible meals for your students. You will. You'll pour your heart into lessons that will become the backbone of your curriculum. But most days, most days, you're putting together something solid and doable. Your students don't need a feast every day, and you don't have the energy to make one.

So don't kill yourself trying to recreate the lessons you did in college for every day of instruction. You'll collect those intricate lessons over time, and they will become the backbone of your curriculum. But it takes time to curate and perfect those lessons, so for now, just work on something manageable.

This isn't about lowering the bar; it's about surviving long enough to do all the things this job demands. So, permit yourself to plan practically, if not perfectly. Let go of the 6-hour nights after school, planning for a 52-minute period. I think you'll find that your students like tacos and burgers just fine, too.

Standard-Based Teaching

You very likely have standards for teaching wherever you are. They may be Common Core or state standards, but you'll have them and need to familiarize yourself with them.

Not every school will handle standards the same way. I've worked in schools where the standard needs to be posted and referred to each class period. I've been at a school where, as long as it was on my lesson plan, I was good to go, and I've even taught at schools where no one even bothered to check and just assumed that I was using standards to teach.

No matter what kind of situation you've found yourself in, the state standards are a decent place to start if you're just trying to figure out what to teach every day.

The standards help you figure out what is important to teach and where you need to go. If the standards are your map, the objective is your route.

> If the standards are your map, the objective is your route.

From Standard to Objective

When you're looking at a standard, you're reading it to find out what students should know or be able to do that they didn't know and couldn't do before being taught the standard.

Let's take a look at a fifth-grade standard for English Language Arts from the Common Core:

CCSS.ELA-Literacy.L.5.4 Vocabulary Acquisition and Use

Determine or clarify the meaning of unknown and multiple-meaning words and phrases based on grade 5 reading and content, choosing flexibly from a range of strategies:

a. Use context (e.g., cause/effect relationships and comparisons in text) as a clue to the meaning of a word or phrase.
b. Use common, grade-appropriate Greek and Latin affixes and roots as clues to the meaning of a word (e.g., *photograph, photosynthesis*).
c. Consult reference materials (e.g., dictionaries, glossaries, thesauruses), both print and digital, to find the pronunciation and determine or clarify the precise meaning of key words and phrases.

Source: Common Core State Standards Initiative, 2010

This is a pretty routine Common Core standard. But looking at it you now have free rein to build your lesson however you want, provided you're making sure students can do what the standard is asking.

So, what is the standard asking? It wants students to be able to determine or clarify the meaning of specific words. So those are the verbs we'll be using: determine and clarify.

That is going into your objective. Depending on where you teach, you will have various conventions for objectives, but the most common are the "students will be able to…" and "I can…" I started using "I can" a while back and just stuck with it, but feel free to use either if you're allowed to; they do the same thing, and there really isn't a lot of data that supports one over the other, but getting an objective on the board is key here.

Anyway, here's what we have for an objective so far: "I can determine the meaning of unknown words and phrases." That's pretty rock solid and will allow us to craft a lesson from there.

Looking at the rest of the standard, we see that they want to use context clues, grade-appropriate Greek and Latin affixes and roots, and/or consult reference materials. If no one has ever told you this, you do not have to teach all of the standards in one lesson, and you do not have to fit it all in one day. You could stretch this standard out over several lessons and even revisit it later when appropriate.

If we were focusing on part A, we might write our objective as such: "I can determine the meaning of unknown words or phrases using context clues."

If we wanted to do part B, our objective might be "Students will be able to determine the meaning of words using Greek and Latin affixes and roots."

Lastly, if you were doing part C, the objective might read "I can use reference materials to determine the meaning of key words or phrases."

They don't have to be magical objectives, just enough to let the students (and any nosy administrators walking by) know what they should be able to do by the end of the lesson. To put it another way, what is the new skill they can show off? Can they now go home to mom and dad and say, "Look, I can use Greek suffixes to determine the meaning of words!" I know no one talks like that, but that is a demonstrable skill, so voilà, a solid objective.

> ### An Aside on Lesson Planning
>
> Some great lesson ideas started out scribbled on a sticky note or a napkin or while I was drinking my morning coffee, brushing my teeth, or sitting on the can. Inspiration does not arrive on schedule. It shows up sometimes when you least expect it. Some of my most impactful lessons were not created in a vacuum by myself. They were co-created with colleagues, and my best lessons were made with people who didn't teach what I did.
>
> Teaching is creative work, and creative work doesn't always respect the boundaries of your prep period. Not to mention the speed at which things happen in the world may force you to adjust your plans at the last minute.
>
> Early in my career, I built a Declaration of Independence lesson with a math teacher friend who helped me break down abstract concepts in a way that actually landed with my kids. Another great lesson I created came from spitballing ideas over falafel with my friend, who taught special education.
>
> My point is, starting with the standard is great, but what actually goes into the lesson can, and likely will, come from anywhere.

Writing Better Objectives

Okay, now that we've covered how to pull an objective from a standard, let's look at writing effective learning objectives. Sure, I showed you some examples, but I didn't really explain what I was doing. I have seen so many lessons where the learning objective sounds good, but doesn't really say anything.

Sometimes, teachers will write that students will "know" or "understand" something, and that's great if they do, but how are you measuring knowing or understanding? What are students doing to demonstrate that they know or understand? Objectives need to be clearly measurable.

Where can we find out which verbs make sense for the lesson? For that, we'll refer to our old friend Bloom and his famous taxonomy. You no doubt have seen or heard of him and his work before, definitely during your college prep courses. If you're not familiar with it, strap in, buckaroo, you're about to get verb rocked.

Bloom's Taxonomy is a series of verbs that move from simple to more complex as the demands of brain work increase as well (Bloom et al., 1956; Anderson & Krathwohl, 2001).

Bloom's original taxonomy moved from Evaluation to Knowledge, basically, students really thinking about a topic vs. simple recall. However, in 2001, it was reworked to be Remember, Understand, Apply, Analyze, Evaluate, and Create (Anderson & Krathwohl, 2001). Every learning objective doesn't need to be a "create," but if you find yourself stuck in a rut, you might want to consult this list.

Wait a minute! Didn't I just say not to use "understand" in a learning objective? I did, and I still stand by it. Unless you're giving an exam of some kind, you're not really going to be able to measure understanding, and you're better off using a different verb, like "diagram" or "describe" than understand.

Let's look at a learning objective that sucks and make it suck less, while still accomplishing the same goal.

Sucky Objective
Students will understand how the US Constitution creates a system of checks and balances.

Less Sucky Objective
Students will be able to diagram the system of checks and balances created by the US Constitution by accurately labeling checks among the branches of government.

See the difference?

The first one could mean anything, but by stating specifically how students will demonstrate their understanding, we now have an end goal from which to work backward.

> **Another Aside about Lesson Planning**
>
> The worst lessons I've taught in my life were ones where I didn't have a clear learning objective. When I wasn't sure what I wanted kids to do, things fell apart. If you go in with only a vague sense of what students should accomplish, they will walk away with only a vague sense of learning.
>
> Not to mention, students are worse behaved, in my experience, when the lesson is not fully developed. They can sense it, and they will know you're unsure of where you're leading them, and they will not want to follow blindly.
>
> So do yourself a favor and take time to write a strong learning objective. That is where everything starts. When my wife was a biology teacher, she would ask me for help writing her lessons, and she would say, "What should I do tomorrow?" and I would ask her every time, "What is your objective?" and she usually wouldn't have one, but once we were able to develop one, the lesson grew naturally from that.

From Objective to Activities

Now that we've established a clear understanding of learning objectives (I hope), we can work backwards to figure out what the lesson should look like.

If students will be able to do X by the end of the lesson, you'll need to ask yourself, "What do they need to be able to do to do X?" Likely, it is "Y," and from there you can find "Z," which is more actionable than winging it.

Let's return to the less sucky objective from earlier:

Students will be able to diagram the system of checks and balances created by the US Constitution by accurately labeling checks among the branches of government.

Okay, so the last thing students will do is diagram the system of checks and balances among the branches. What do they need to know before that? They need to know what checks and balances exist, so I'll need them to learn that. But before that, they'll need an understanding of what a check is and what it means to "balance" each other with regard to the three branches of government. Even before that, we need to introduce, or at least make sure the students know, that there are three branches of government.

If we look at this in order, it would go like this:

1. Three branches of government.
2. What are checks and balances?
3. What checks and balances exist?
4. Diagram the system of checks and balances.

Now that we have the framework, we can figure out how best to plan this lesson with activities that will engage the students.

The Teaching Spiral

So, how do we move from "here is what students should know or do" to actually lesson planning? That is where what I call the Teaching Spiral comes in. Trademarked. Okay, not really. Also, not sure if I can say that if it isn't, but that sounds like a problem for the editor.

In order to figure out what kind of activities we're going to use, we'll need to figure out where those activities land in the overall scope of the lesson plan. You could very well just lecture to students for 90% of your class and then say, "Here, draw a diagram," but that would be a pretty crappy lesson. Students need to be engaged, and good learning always has and always will move from teacher-focused to student-focused. There are variations on the theme, but the heart stays the same.

I'm going to talk you through how I lesson plan and what works for me. Take it, use it, modify it, remix it, do what works best for you, but if you are still getting stuck every day or lessons are feeling like they are just not it, this might be the plug-and-play you're looking for.

14 ◆ Suck Less in the Classroom Tomorrow

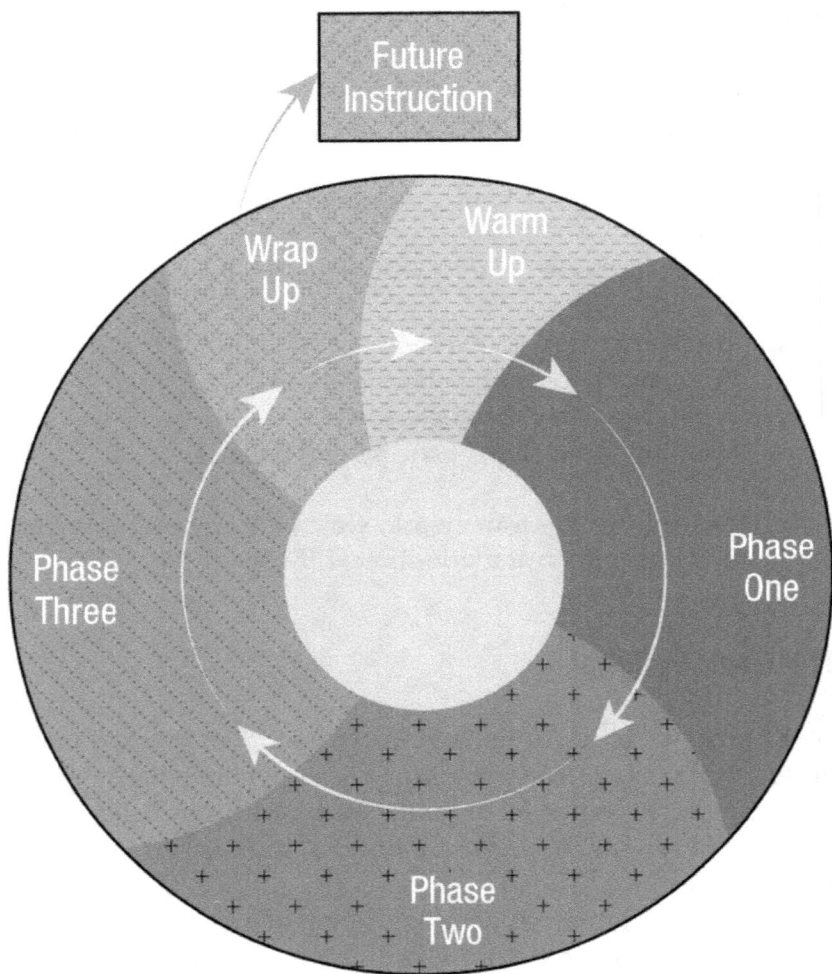

FIGURE 2.1 The Teaching Spiral

The Spiral Explained

I've split my plan into five distinct parts, drawing from the *Gradual Release of Responsibility* model (Fisher & Frey, 2008) and Dr. Zaretta Hammond's framework from *Culturally Responsive Teaching and the Brain* (2015). I've adapted and modified the flow of their models while keeping the core themes intact. Giving credit where credit is due, I've modified their approaches to fit the everyday needs of the classroom and provided a cyclical element that will better inform lesson planning.

The *Gradual Release* uses the framework of "I Do, We Do, You Do" while Dr. Hammond's framework moves from Ignite, to Chunk, to Chew, to Review.

The Teaching Spiral is named because it comes back onto itself. Don't worry, I'll explain in a bit, but I don't want to get ahead of myself.

The five parts of the *Teaching Spiral* are Warm-Up, Phase 1—teacher-focused instruction, Phase 2—student-centered learning, Phase 3—independent practice, and Wrap-Up. This standard practice might even be something you're familiar with. However, if you're like I was when I first started teaching, you might believe that all learning and instruction must come from the teacher, but I'm here to tell you that not only is that not entirely true, it is the least sustainable way of teaching.

To get a feel for what this might look like, let's take a step into a kitchen:

Scene: Interior Kitchen

Two adults are making food.

CHILD:	What are you making?
ADULT:	We're making food.
CHILD:	I want to make food too!
ADULT 1:	Okay, let me show you.
ADULT 1:	Here, this is how you do it.

The adults take the materials and models how to make whatever they're making. They might make a few for them to see.

ADULT 1:	See how I do the thing that makes these into the thing they are?
CHILD:	Uh-huh.
ADULT 2:	Okay, now you try.
CHILD:	Okay.

The child tries, probably poorly at first, not taking the time to do it well and/or lacking the proficiency from years of making the food.

What happens next? Do you think the adults would sit there and allow the child to fail at making food important to them? No, of course not.

ADULT 1:   Not bad for your first time. But here, try this.

Time passes, and the child makes several more attempts. Eventually, the child is proficient enough to make the food without the watchful eye of the adults. However, the adults are there to help if the child falters.

After many more attempts, the child can pull it off.

ADULTS: Terrific, you've done it!
CHILD: Yay! I am the non-specific traditionally ethnic food-making royal person!

They enjoy the food together, and the child tells of their triumphs in the kitchen.

So that's the Teaching Spiral in a nutshell. Curiosity sparked, instruction modeled, guided practice, independence, and celebration or closing. Just like in a kitchen or a classroom, learning is a shared experience as we move toward mastery.

Warm-Up

Some call this a "do now," others a "bellringer," some just "bell work," but regardless of what you call it, what are your kids going to do when they walk into class? The goal for this block is for it to take no more than 10% of your class time. So, if you have 45–60-minute periods, that's about 5 minutes. If you have 90-minute blocks, maybe you stretch it out and call on a few more students to share their answers.

I've seen many teachers skip the Warm-Up and just jump straight into the lesson. This can be jarring for students who aren't always prepared to learn yet. Think of the Warm-Up like stretching before you exercise. Not that anyone is going to pull a muscle, but you've got to get the blood flowing first.

To Grade or Not to Grade?

I've done both. If a class isn't taking the warm-up seriously, then yeah—I grade it. It's one of those Catch-22 situations: if you won't do the work, it goes in the gradebook; but if everyone's on point, I don't have to bother. I know that feels like making it a punishment, but Warm-Ups aren't free time, and students should be doing them.

It's really up to you. If you're a teacher who gives participation points or just needs to pad the stats, grade away.

But, in an ideal world, you shouldn't need to grade it.

This is usually something to keep them busy while you deal with all the crap your job makes you do that isn't teaching. Taking attendance, glancing at Slack, checking dress code (if you have one), and maybe collecting homework (which is part of your job, but you know what I mean).

Students are people, and people tend to like predictability. By starting class the same way each day, you are giving them that structure they need to be successful. From a *Culturally Responsive Teaching* standpoint, this routine is useful for students to feel safe. It also allows them to Warm-Up their brains for the learning ahead. They need this low-risk ramp to prepare to receive the rest of the lesson.

Routine is safe.

Routine is calm.

Routine good. No routine bad.

> **Beware of This Teaching Trap**
>
> Open-ended questions are great. I love them. They get students thinking. But they can be a trap. I've observed many lessons in which a starter question spurred a 30-minute conversation that wasn't on the agenda. If you want to plan for that, that's great, but if you didn't, you risk derailing your lesson.

What Makes a Good Starter Question?

I usually use it to review what students should have learned in the previous lesson, not like an exit slip, but more like an entry slip. A formative assessment to see if students got anything from the day before.

Another good strategy is to make the bellringer a little preview of the lesson to see what students know before you start talking about it. Maybe you ask something and get blank stares from everyone, but at least you got them thinking about it and primed the proverbial pump.

Circling back to earlier, this is the part of the lesson that should lead into the hook for the day, which will be the start of Phase 1.

Engaging Students

However you plan your Warm-Up or start of your lesson, you should have a hook.

A hook can be anything that gets the students into the lesson. Maybe it's a TikTok video, or a provocative question (I know you just asked them a question; this is different. A Warm-Up is to get started, a hook is to get going.), it could be a short video from YouTube or an episode of Crash Course, whatever it is, it should lead into your instruction and whet the palate so to speak for the students.

The internet is your friend here, and there are tons of hook ideas out there. You're not the first person to teach what you're teaching, so you should feel empowered to look at what's out there and take what works for you.

Good Hook, Bad Lesson

A good hook is meaningless if your lesson sucks.

Influenced by Hollywood portrayal of teachers and being a college student, I thought I had the perfect plan to show my students just how dedicated to teaching I was and just how exciting history could be.

During my student teaching, for a lesson on World War II, I went all out.

As students entered the room, the lights went out. There was a strobe light flashing while the battle sounds from Saving Private Ryan played on the TV. Then I appeared from a side room. I came out wearing a full military uniform, complete with helmet and face paint, and started shouting at the students.

The students were in shock. They all seemed to be engaged.

Until the lesson began.

I didn't have a lesson. What I had was a gimmick and a slide deck. After I got their attention, I proceeded to give notes on World War II for the next 60 minutes.

Sure, I did it in uniform—but notes are notes. And by the end of the class, everyone was zoned out, and some students fell asleep.

The heart of the matter is: having a great hook will only get you so far, and can't really save you if your lesson is boring as hell.

Phase 1: Getting the Ball Rolling

Phase 1 is where the teacher takes the wheel. Phase 1 is anytime the bulk of the new learning is coming from you, and students are less active participants. Think of Phase 1 like laying the foundation or the groundwork for the lesson.

It doesn't mean the students are just bumps on a log. This just means the locus of control for the lesson is with the teacher. It's your job to get the students ready for what comes next.

If we return to our learning objective (don't worry, I'll put it below so you don't feel bad about forgetting it), we should get an idea of what we need to do as teachers.

Students will be able to diagram the system of checks and balances created by the US Constitution by accurately labeling checks among the branches of government.

Earlier we stated that students need to know about the three branches of government. We would want to review this with students before moving on to the next piece, which should be the new learning of the lesson.

Next, we said they should know what checks and balances are. This could be a lecture, this could be a reading done as a class, this could be a video; it's up to you, but somehow, you're going to use your skill of analogies and metaphors and real-life situations to get your students to understand the new concepts.

Phase 1 should only take about 25% of your period, so if you're just giving guided notes or something, that is fine too; it won't be that long. This can be accomplished in a variety of ways, which have been touched on, but when you picture teaching, what you're usually picturing is Phase 1 stuff. You're probably not picturing walking around the room while your class completes worksheets or takes tests. You're thinking about taking what is in your brain and getting it into their brains.

Phase 1 Instructional Examples:

Phase 1—Teacher-Focused Instruction (≈25%)

- Mini-lecture with Guided Notes: Deliver content with students filling in a note sheet as you go. Guided notes really help to speed things up. Also, students will want to write down everything on a slide if you let them. Nobody has time for that.
- Teacher Think-Aloud: Model your own thought process as you analyze a text or solve a problem.
- Short Anchor Video: Show a video, but for Pete's sake, make sure you're pausing it and explaining and/or clarifying concepts along the way. Don't just let it roll for 15 minutes.
- Demonstration: Walk through step-by-step what students will be asked to do. Model for them and be sure to highlight areas of misconception or mistakes.
- Analogy or Story: Use a real-world example for students to make sense of new learning. Connecting new learning to what we've previously learned or know is an essential step in learning.

A Good Rule of Thumb

Someone told me this one time, and it has proven mostly true in my experience, so I'm passing it along. It's more teacher experience than researched fact, but in general, students can really only sit through lectures or notes at about a minute per year of age. As they get older, it probably is more like 1.5 minutes, but in general, if you're teaching eighth grade, you want to only deliver new content from direct instruction for about 13 minutes. Sure, you can give or take a few minutes there, but if you're giving more than 15 minutes of notes, you're losing the students.

This means for little ones you want to limit direct instruction even less, but could get to around 20 minutes for seniors in high school.

This is in total chunks, not total. So, if you give 15 minutes of notes, but then switch to an activity, and then switch back to notes, you should be able to buy yourself a little more time.

Phase 2: The Heart of the Lesson

This is the heart of the lesson. This is where the guided practice comes in and what should lead to success for students as they transition to Phase 3. *Phase 2 is all about student-centered learning.* What does that mean? It means you're passing the reins to the students ... a little bit.

This is the natural progression of learning. It's how we learned from our parents and how our parents learned from theirs. If we kept all the knowledge solely coming from us and never worked it out with our students, then what are we doing?

Remember when I said I planned a lesson with a math teacher? This was my first-year teaching, and I remember thinking that a good lecture was a good lesson. That I could inspire my students with my prose and position in the classroom because that is how I was taught when I was in school. That is how I learned in college in giant lecture halls. That is how I student taught, mostly. So that is what I brought to an eighth-grade class.

Well, turns out, my math teacher friend was much more familiar with having students practice than I was, as it was her purview being a math teacher, and she had me develop the lesson to where the students were now working with me to interpret the Preamble to the Constitution. She suggested that while I present each line, "We the People of the United States" and "In order to form a more perfect union," etc., that I have students rewrite them in their own words, instead of having me tell the students what it meant.

Sure, it makes perfect sense now, but not every teacher coming out of teacher prep school knows that you shouldn't just lecture to the students and that they won't always be inspired by your words.

Anyway, I did what she suggested, and the lesson went very well. Who knew?

If we revisit our objective about diagramming the checks and balances that exist between the branches of government in the United States, we know that we are now at the part of the lesson where students need to learn what checks and balances exist.

Here, you could do some student-centered, but teacher-involved, activities. You might do a guided reading where students read aloud with the class and fill in blanks on a worksheet. You might project excerpts from the Constitution or Federalist Papers and have students pick out the checks that exist. You could do a list-label-group (in the appendix) with the checks that exist, read them, and have students rework their lists from the provided material.

I can't possibly list all the ways to bring students into the fold, but know that for this part of the lesson, you want the students engaged. It could be a four corners activity or some other activity where you get the students moving and thinking, but ultimately, it should be some give and take between teacher and student. This is the part of the lesson where we are watching carefully as they make their non-specific dish in the kitchen, ready to assist if they need a hand.

Resist the urge to take back control here. Remember, we're about to take the training wheels off, so they are going to have to be able to ride on their own.

> ### A Great Spot for Cooperative Learning
>
> This step is also a great place to put in some cooperative learning.
>
> If you're looking to take teamwork in the classroom up a notch, check out the work of Spencer Kagan and the Kagan Cooperative Learning training that is available (I highly recommend it).
>
> Cooperative learning is like group work, but it is structured in a way to provide accountability.
>
> If you were doing said math problems with cooperative learning, you might have one problem and two students, where each student has to do a step of the problem to solve it. In this way, each student is accountable to the other student, but also has a built-in coach as well.
>
> Cooperative learning is a great tool, and a quick search on the internet browser of your choice will return many structures you can plop right into any lesson you've been working on.
>
> I don't love "group work" where there are too many opportunities for "hogs (students who want to do all the work) and logs (students who are okay letting others do all the work)," and using structures like cooperative learning helps to prevent that from happening too much in the classroom.

Phase 2—Student-Centered Practice (≈25%)

- Turn and Talk Discussions: Have students discuss new ideas with a partner before sharing with the whole class (included in the Appendix).
- Guided Reading and/or Annotation: Students read and annotate as they go with teacher guidance and support.

For example, circling unfamiliar words, underlining key concepts.
- Four Corners: Students move to a corner of the room that represents how they feel about a topic and then have to defend themselves or convince others of their position.
- List–Label–Group: Students sort and categorize new words or concepts to build familiarity and meaning (included in the Appendix).
- Cooperative Learning Task: Use predesigned structures to ensure all students are participating and engaging in the learning.

Phase 3: Where the Rubber Hits the Proverbial Road

If Phase 2 is where the real learning takes place, Phase 3 is where students demonstrate that learning. Both the *Gradual Release* model and Dr. Hammond's model have a phase for independent student practice. And if you refer back to our kitchen analogy, this is when things start to really cook (see what I did there?).

In theory, this should be the easiest phase to plan since you've already written an objective that states what students will be doing to demonstrate mastery of the objective.

What does this look like? If we're trying to get students to diagram the checks and balances of the United States, this is where they would create that diagram. I would have the students review their notes from Phase 2, reference what was talked about in Phase 1, and diagram the checks and balances of the United States.

If you were teaching science, this is where students are finishing their labs and creating their reports. If you were teaching a math class, this is when students would independently work on math problems. The crux of this phase, though, is what are students going to do on their own? How are they going to take the new skill and apply it?

Now, this doesn't mean you simply introduce the task and then go back to your desk. You are still there to support students during this phase when they get stuck or falter, but you're ultimately not the source of brain power during this time. The students are doing the work to demonstrate, hopefully, success on today's objective.

This is where you should begin the lesson planning process. Meaning, these are the activities for the lesson you want to plan first, before working on Phase 1 or 2. Once you've written your objective, you should ask the question, "Now what does that look like?" That is how you're going to come to design Phase 3.

> **Pro-Tip: Varying Modalities**
>
> I like to give multiple modes of learning the same important information to students.
>
> So we take a few slides of notes on the Cold War and McCarthyism, and then you have students watch a short video about McCarthyism and its impacts.
>
> Following that, you have a short reading about the trials and "witch hunts" that Ole' Joey McRedscare did before drinking himself to death. Now you've engaged your learners in three modes of getting the same info.
>
> This is critical because even though learning styles have essentially been debunked (Pashler, McDaniel, Rohrer, & Bjork, 2008), we're still fighting for student focus, and the more variety you have to get the info to them, the more likely it is to stick.

Phase 3 can take many forms, from quizzes to short writings. Here are a few that might work for you:

Phase 3—Independent Practice (≈25%)

- ♦ Diagram or Graphic Organizer: Students create a map, or chart, or flow diagram. I really like having students create brochures here and make each of the 6 panels demonstrate a part of the learning.

- Independent Short Write: Students do a short writing to summarize new learning (R.A.F.T. and G.R.A.S.P.S. are good examples and included in the Appendix!).
- Practice Problem Set: Math problems, sentence rewrites, general practice questions—like those found at the end of a chapter in a textbook.
- Case Study: Students apply concepts to a realistic scenario.
- Creative Product: Students create a social media post, poster, image, meme, or some other representation of new learning.

Transitions

Before we wrap up here, we should talk about how you're going to transition between each phase. While they are all distinct, there are five of them, and if you're taking a minute or two moving between each one, you're losing anywhere from five to ten minutes of class time.

Passing Out Materials

Do this during the phase that precedes needing the materials, but without stopping to do it. Meaning, if you're doing a guided notes lecture for Phase 1, you should be passing out the guided notes during the Warm-Up while students are working, or even better, have students pick them up as they enter the room.

It might sound like a no-brainer, like most things about teaching seem, but planning how you're going to distribute needed materials to students is a great thing to preplan. Some teachers have them passed out already, others have a stack for students to grab when they come in, and some practice having rows pass them out. There are so many ways to get materials to students, and it is a low lift, high yield, to figure that out before the lesson starts.

Moving Desks

If you need desks in a certain arrangement before the lesson starts, you'll be able to do that before students arrive, however if you need to do it during the lesson, you'll need a plan. I had a teacher I worked with who would practice this with her students to make it go as quickly as possible. When she would say "transform," the students would quickly move from rows into groups of four, and she would give out candy to the group that got there first. By practicing it beforehand and providing an incentive, this activity was cut to mere seconds of class time.

Switching to Devices

If you're moving on to a Kahoot or something similar, you can project the code early so students can start logging in as they are finishing up their work. For example, if you're using a Kahoot for your Wrap-Up, you can project the code they need while they are doing Phase 3. This way, you're only waiting on a handful when it is time to go.

Those are just a few things that might slow you down with transitions. I also just like to move straight to the next thing without letting students come up for air. It's just "okay, now I need you to…" I don't indicate we're moving on; I just give the next direction and have them catch up.

Wrap-Up

This is the final part of the lesson. Here is where you need to tie things up and find out what the students learned. This is also the part of the lesson that will inform your future lessons, maybe even tomorrow's lesson. The style of a Wrap-Up can vary depending on what you're doing, but it should be intentional and give you a pulse check on what the class, or at least, most of the class, knows.

What are some ways to accomplish a Wrap-Up?

Well, the simplest ways are probably the least effective but still valuable. You could take a thumbs up, thumb to the side, or thumb down pulse check. If everyone gives the thumbs up, you know you can move on to the next lesson. If you get a lot of sideways or thumbs down, though, it is likely time to reteach or review key concepts.

Another quick and easy Wrap-Up is an emoji Wrap-Up, or maybe you've seen the memes of which "x" are you, where students pick a picture that reflects how they are feeling about the lesson.

You could use an electronic device or website such as Poll Everywhere, Plickers, Kahoot, Blooket, Socrative, or Quizizz. There are likely more than those, and new ones are coming out all the time. Some of these lend themselves to older students more than younger, but they should be accessible for most age groups.

Using any of the above sites will take some work, as you may have to write the questions, create an account, and figure out how to distribute it to the students, but I've used them all, and they are all effective ways to Wrap-Up. You'd be surprised what you can learn from a five-question Kahoot for a pulse check.

If you want something a little more concrete and independent you could do a more formal exit ticket. An exit ticket can take many forms; it could be a Google Form or some other quick questioning software, but it will likely be a slip of paper where the students need to answer a question.

One way to do an exit ticket is to just ask an open-ended question related to the day's lessons. Another way is obviously to ask a closed question where there is one right answer. An example of this might be demonstrating a shift in a demand curve based on a scenario, after the students have been practicing it during the period.

I've heard of some cool other ways to assess the lesson and put a bow on it, and I'll list them down below:

- The "2 Dollar" exit slip. Each word costs ten cents, and students need to summarize the day's learning.
- Make a tweet. Students get 140 or 280 characters (or thereabout) to summarize the day's learning.
- Write a haiku reflecting what they have gathered from today.
- Snowball quiz—this is covered in the Appendix, so I won't go over it again here, sorry.
- Sticky note out the door. Students answer a prompt or question on a Sticky note and literally stick it to the door as they leave.

- A 3-2-1 summary. You can have them be anything, but it could be 3 things they learned, 2 things they still wonder about, and 1 thing they already knew. You can mix and match them and make up new things, such as 1 thing they wonder or 2 things that connect to the world today.
- Summary Compass. North—New Learning. South—Something surprising. East—Evidence from the lesson. West—Something they wonder about.

However you plan to Wrap-Up the lesson, none of it matters if you don't use the information gained to inform your instruction.

Did most of your students miss some key piece of the lesson? You need a reteach. Did they all ace your exit slip? Time to quiz or move on, or both! If only a few students are still confused, what can you do to support them? How about if only one student gets the lesson? What are they going to do while you're reteaching?

This is why it is called the Teaching Spiral. Your lessons inform one another. The Warm-Up sets the stage for Phase 1, which sets up students to work in Phase 2. This leads to the independent practice of Phase 3, and ultimately allows students to answer the questions from the Wrap-Up, which in turn informs future instruction.

Formative vs. Summative Assessments

Before we move on, it's worth clarifying the difference between a formative and a summative assessment, and when you might use each.

A formative assessment is like a pulse check. The Wrap-Ups I've described above are mostly formative assessments. They inform instruction. They allow you to see what students know and how they are doing in real time and then make adjustments from there. If you ask students thumbs up or thumbs down, how are they doing, and you get a whole lotta thumbs down, you're going to need to stop and reassess how you're teaching. You might have to scrap tomorrow's lesson and reteach, differently, what they are learning today. That's okay, though. The students are the consumers of our product, and we want to make sure they're learning at the end of the day, not just sticking to some timetable.

Whereas a summative assessment is something you give at the end of instruction. I tend to do them at the end of units of instruction, but you can do them whenever it seems appropriate. A quiz after a day or two of learning is a summative assessment; a homework assignment can be a summative assessment. There are many that you can choose from, but in general, think of them as quizzes, tests, and longer writing prompts.

When in doubt, ask yourself, "Do I need information to decide where to go next?" If so, that's formative. "Am I assessing the sum of what students have learned?" That's summative.

Summative assessment do inform instruction and let us know how we have been teaching and what students have been learning, but they are more "lag measures" in that by the time we get the results, it is too late to really go back and reteach. But all assessments are informative for our practice.

Writing Good Questions

One thing I learned in my time as an instructional coach is that teachers overestimate their ability to create great questions on the fly. We assume, since we know our content, we'll be able to pull information from our students on a whim, and thus we don't need to prepare questions in advance.

For the advanced orators out there and seasoned teachers, this might be true, but for the rest of us, we need to prepare our questions in advance.

When you're writing your lessons, a hack I've made is to create three types of questions to assess various levels of learning.

Here is a simple framework that will help you cover a range of skills.

Write a retrieval question; these *are* the questions that we tend toward naturally while teaching, but it is still a good idea to pre-write this ahead of time.

Create a question that forces students to draw connections between what they are learning and what they have previously learned. Connecting new learning to previous learning makes it more "sticky" for students (Willingham, 2009). It's like knowing how to play one card game and it being easier for you to play another card game, like *Go Fish* and *Old Maid*. Have students make those connections.

Design a synthesis question. If you recall Bloom's from earlier, this is on the higher order of thinking. You want students to take new learning and apply it in interesting and new ways.

Someone once told me, "Never ask a question you don't want every student to answer." That doesn't mean you have to call on every student, but good questioning means giving each student time to think about the answer, or literally having them all write the answer down so they are all doing the processing.

How you ask questions can vary as well, and should. Maybe you ask your retrieval question during Phase 1 and have your connection question in the middle of Phase 2, and give your synthesis question during independent practice. Or you could build them all off each other and do it rapid fire.

However, you do it, trust me on pre-writing your questions. It'll lead to a more engaged classroom and give you more information on what students are learning.

The Teaching Spiral in Practice

So, you have to teach something tomorrow, and you're not sure what. Here is how you can use this in some easy steps and how I go about thinking about lesson planning:

1. What is the objective? (You might have to use the standard here as well, but honestly, that is school dependent. Most

of the time, something you're teaching will hit one of the standards for your subject.)
2. How will you know students mastered the objective? (Phase 3)
3. What do students need to do to get there? (Phase 2)
4. What do students need to know from me? (Phase 1)
5. What will students do when they walk into the door? (Warm-Up)
6. How will I bring all of this to a close? (Wrap-Up)

If you follow that line of planning, lesson planning will flow naturally from the objective, and you'll be able to make lessons that reach students and keep their interest.

After the Lesson

Once the lesson is taught and the students are gone, now what? Do we simply move on to the next day? Hopefully, no. If you are lucky enough to be teaching the same thing next year, you'll want to make changes now while it is fresh in your mind and not try and remember in a year after a long summer.

After the lesson, go back to your planning document and make a note at the bottom. This doesn't have to take very long, just a quick three to five minutes while you wait for the buses to leave is enough to make a big impact. Make changes to your slides now, not later. I know it seems like a big lift when you're exhausted at the end of the day but Future You will thank you.

Questions to consider:

- What really worked in this lesson?
- What questions did students have?
- How did the Wrap-Up go? Did all the students know the answers? Did none of them know?
- What was clunky or redundant on the slides? Is there anything they don't actually need to know that you can cut?

- What would you have done differently if you had to teach this lesson again tomorrow?

When to Not Use the Teaching Spiral

Not every lesson will lend itself to the Teaching Spiral. Some days you might be showing a movie, or students are doing presentations, or writing an essay. There will be days when you will have to modify the structure to fit your needs. If you're giving a test that day, don't think you have to fit it into Phase 3 and still do the other phases that day. I know this should go without saying, but while I believe that most lessons will fit well into the format, obviously, the nature of the job will ensure that deviations will happen.

Differentiation

We should take a second to address the elephant in the room. In today's educational landscape, you will be asked to differentiate your lessons based on individual education plans. I've been doing this a while, have taught in four different states and nearly twice as many schools, and I can say that most of the accommodations that students receive are fairly common across the board. Meaning, that many students will get notes, or information broken down into chunks, etc. Very rarely will you have a child with a unique learning scaffold that is unlike any other that is out there. That is in no way to downplay the needs of individual students; it is simply to say that many students will benefit from similar support.

The best way to address this, without having to plan 30 different lessons, is to build the accommodations into your lesson.

If a student is supposed to get a graphic organizer to use during instruction, create a graphic organizer for everyone. It'll save you time, meet the needs of your student, and everyone can benefit from this added scaffold. If a student is allowed to use notes on a test, you could allow all students to use notes if it isn't that disruptive.

My point is, every time you're able to take the modification or scaffold and add it into your lesson, such as planning to present things in chunks, you're covering your bases, and it's okay if all students benefit from it.

When planning for shortened or modified assignments, you will need to plan for that in advance, but taking things off a plate is always easier than putting them on.

What about High Flyers?

Differentiation isn't only about the students who need more help; it is also about the students who need a little more. Inevitably, you will have students who are not as challenged by the work or finish early every time there is an assignment. Here are a few ways to address them that I have found to work:

- ♦ Challenge questions—add one or two questions to your assignments that are there as "challenge questions"; no one has to do them, but if you do, you'll get a little more feedback, challenge yourself, and maybe a bonus point or two (if you're into that).
- ♦ Independent Projects—give students who finish early something else to work on that allows them to creatively use their time in class. Maybe it is an extra report, a slide deck, or a poster project, but something to allow them to stretch what they've been learning.
- ♦ Peer Tutor—this is a simple "oh you're done? Can you go help someone else?" This gets them out of the seat and interacting with other students, which is a good way to prevent disruptive boredom.
- ♦ Read a book—it's never been said that our students read too much. If students finish early and just do not

want to work on something else, help a peer, or do the extra questions, you can always have them read a book. I keep a little library in my classroom just for these occasions.
- ♦ Special Assignment—when all else fails, I will find something for them to do, like organize a table in my room, water my plants, or run something to the office. It's not ideal, but at least they're moving.

At the end of the day, the goal here is engagement and preventing students from distracting others because they are bored and need to put their energy somewhere.

Unit Planning

Unit planning is where your standards are really going to come into play. Here you'll want to look at everything you have to teach, figure out what you can reasonably get through, and then organize the standards as best you can into related chunks.

An example, from the US Government, might be Unit 1: Foundations of Government (Constitution, Origins of Government, Types of Governments, etc.), Unit 2: The Legislative Branch (Congress, Passing Laws, etc.), Unit 3: The Executive Branch (Presidents, Elections, Bureaucracy), and Unit 4: The Judicial Branch and Civil Rights. That is one way to split up a course that is usually one semester, or nine weeks long.

Four to five units per semester are ideal. If you teach year-long courses or elementary school, your units may be longer or you might just have more, but for my money, four to five seems to be the right amount.

The reality is, any district that has you submit lesson plans is going to ask where in the unit it falls. You're going to need to figure that out if you're in one of those districts or schools. Ideally, you'll be given time to figure that out at the start of the school year, and in some cases, especially for the tested subjects, you'll be given a curriculum map by the school as well.

If you're not given anything, don't fret. That just means you have the freedom to create the plan as you go and figure it out. Sure, that seems daunting, but when you can revisit your plans and make personal adjustments, it is liberating not to have to meet someone else's timeline.

95% Rule

Don't plan for every single minute, at least not until you've mastered the 95% rule. The 95% rule simply means to plan 95% of your lesson. So, if you have 90-minute blocks, you're going to plan 86 (rounding) minutes of instruction. I've heard another way is to "leave room for wonder," but what you're doing here is leaving room for Murphy's Law. Anything that can go wrong will go wrong. That could be a technology issue, a student redirection, a call from the office, any sort of issue could throw your lesson off by a few minutes, and if you've planned bell to bell, you're going to have to cut something. Unfortunately, in my experience, the thing that gets cut is either the Wrap-Up—where students bring their learning to a close, or part of Phase 3—where students make sense of their learning and demonstrate mastery, neither of which you want to cut, but they come at the end of the lesson and are the first to go.

This is definitely a "trust me now and believe me later" situation, but until you've mastered your craft and taught the lesson a few times, there's no need to plan every single second, plan 95%, and you'll see how quickly that fills up the time.

No Free Time

On the days when everything goes as planned, and you're left with a few extra minutes with nothing to do, this is where you can do some relationship building. While students are finishing their Wrap-Up, and you see the clock says they will have extra time, you can start going around and talking to your students. Find out who plays a sport, what shows they are watching, and if they have any pets. Just ask them questions, and you'd be surprised how quickly those handful of minutes fly by.

If that's not your style, use this time to clean up the room or straighten their desks up. You can do a quick temperature check or review the Wrap-Up or independent work with them.

Lastly, if you notice you have that extra time and things are running smoothly, no student is going to complain about having a few extra minutes to work on their assignment (and some might actually need it).

So, what does this look like? Here is a simple rundown of how I would plan my lesson following the 95% rule:

Section	Percent of Period (%)	What Does It Look Like?
Warm-Up	10	Bellringer, taking attendance, getting students settled
Phase 1	25	Hook, chunking instruction, teacher-led
Phase 2	25	Student-centered, teacher-guided, working out new learning collaboratively
Phase 3	25	Independent practice or review, students apply new learning on their own
Wrap-Up	10	Pulse check, closing of lesson, determining what will be taught in future lessons

Templates

Using a lesson plan template is an easy way for you to stay consistent and guide your thinking. Yes, I have written my fair share of lessons on sticky notes, and you do you, as they say. But I still recommend finding a template that works for you.

Here is an example of a lesson plan template you can use for planning:

Sample Lesson Template

Standard:	
Objective:	
Warm-Up:	Phase 1:
Wrap-Up:	
Phase 3:	Phase 2:
Questions: Retrieval: Connection: Synthesis:	

FIGURE 2.2 Blank Lesson Template

Using what we've completed so far, here is what a lesson might look like in practice:

Standard: HS.4 Examine institutions, functions and processes of the United States government.	
Objective: Students will be able to diagram the system of checks and balances created by the US Constitution by accurately labeling checks among the branches of government.	
Warm-Up: Students will answer the question: What are the three branches of government and what are the distinct roles they have in the United States federal government?	**Phase 1:** Hook: Imagine the President said they were going to ban TikTok without any input from Congress? What might happen? How would you react to this? Students will view a short (5 min) video about checks and balances. Students will then take notes comparing different types of checks, and highlight in their Constitutions where those checks exist.
Wrap-Up: Exit Ticket: Students will complete a matching activity matching the correct check to the correct branch of government and then answer the question "what could happen is each branch was not able to limit the power of the other branches?"	
Phase 3: Students will diagram the three branches of government and their checks on one another. For example, "Congress can override a Presidential veto" with a line connecting Congress to the President.	**Phase 2:** Selected guided-reading. Students will examine excerpts from the Federalist papers, Supreme Court rulings, and resources from iCivics online to create a list of checks and balances that exist.
Questions: Where are the powers denied to Congress located? Have you ever seen a time when the Courts have prevented the President from doing something? Why would it have been important to the Framers to build in the system of checks and balances?	

FIGURE 2.3 Completed Lesson Template

Where Do Lesson Ideas Come From?

Now that we've covered *how to teach*, you might still be struggling with *what to teach*. For that, I've included some advice below that you may or may not already have thought about.

Using the Textbook

There is no shame in using the textbook. However, there is also a huge difference between teaching from the textbook and teaching the textbook. Teaching the textbook is going page by page and resource by resource. Teaching from the textbook involves using it to inform your planning and lessons. Using the information provided in the textbook to inform your lesson planning is a solid strategy for creating lessons when you get stuck.

I do want to say that textbooks are usually created using the standards and are *generally* (See *Lies My Teacher Told Me* by James Loewen) a safe place to find information. Don't let a veteran teacher shame you away from using the resources provided for you.

Textbooks also add a little air of validity to what you're teaching. If you give notes in Phase 1 on something and then in Phase 2, students are reading about it in their textbooks they're sometimes like "oh, he wasn't making this up!"

Also, if you remember what I said about varying modalities, it's not bad to use a few pages from the textbook to reinforce some learning.

However, if you're at one of those schools that doesn't have textbooks, I've got you covered, too.

Help Is a Keyboard Away

If you're still stuck trying to come up with lesson plan ideas, I have reviewed some of the common ways to come up with plans below:

Teaching with AI

It's not cheating when you do it. Seriously. Using AI to teach isn't cutting corners—it's just the way things are going. There are so many AI tools out there for teachers that I'm not even going to list them. (Besides, by the time you read this, they'll probably have changed names—or been replaced by something newer and better.)

Using AI is like putting the collective knowledge of the internet to work for you. It's been trained on countless lesson plans, teaching strategies, and yes, even Wikipedia. It knows a lot—and it's fast.

Here are a few specific ways I use AI:

- **Starter questions**: Sometimes I just can't think of a good opener to get kids thinking. So, I ask AI for five ideas. I don't always use them, but it gets my brain going.
- **Rubrics**: Letting AI generate basic rubrics is a huge time-saver. Most rubrics follow a familiar format—from "Exceeds Expectations" to "Needs Work"—so there's no need to reinvent the wheel every time.
- **Assignment directions**: Another big time-saver. I input the prompt, goal, and requirements, and let AI write a clean, student-facing description.
- **Lesson outlines and resources**: I put this last because it's where AI can be hit or miss. It sometimes suggests resources that don't exist or are way too long and boring. Remember, AI doesn't know your students—it's solving the problem like a machine. Still, the outlines are usually helpful, and you can often find real resources by googling what the AI suggests (even if you don't use the exact things it gives you).

The Treasure Trove of Lesson Plans That Is the Internet

There is no need to reinvent the wheel. As Harry Wong might say, a good teacher should "beg, borrow, and steal." I think I would modify his phrase for the modern world to "beg, borrow, steal, and buy."

A quick internet search will usually return several sites that already host what you're teaching. If someone else is teaching the same standards or topic, they have likely developed a very similar plan to what you had, or better yet, a better plan (because maybe you didn't have a plan, which is why you're online looking). Take it. Take the plan you find online, but be sure to read through it first (or, for God's sake, at least skim it) and make sure it works for you.

I once spent an entire evening writing a lesson where I taught the Declaration of Independence as a break-up letter. I had all this stuff built into it about how it was the colonists dumping the King, and then I was going to have the students write their own break-up letter to the king using the Declaration. Then I went online a year later, and it turns out that many, many teachers teach it this way, and there are even videos of this lesson on YouTube. My point is, other teachers are smart, and they probably have good ideas, so see what's out there.

Work smarter, not harder.

Buying Lesson Plans

When AI and the internet have let you down, buy a lesson plan. Teachers Pay Teachers (TPT) has got me out of a jam more than once. I often find lessons that are almost exactly what I was going to do anyway, and I've decided it's worth a few dollars to save myself a few hours. It's just simple math. One nice thing about sites like TPT is that the lessons are often vetted by other teachers who are in the same boat as you. There's no shame in buying a lesson if it helps you get through the week and gives you a night off.

Sub Plans/Emergency Plans

Here's where AI, the internet, and TPT can be your best friends. Many schools require teachers to submit emergency sub plans—and unless you're intentionally making someone's life harder, you should be submitting plans for when you're out.

Sub plans should be something students can do independently, with little input from the teacher. If you're at the primary level, your plans will naturally require more teacher involvement.

But once students have different teachers for different subjects—like math and ELA—you should be creating sub plans that students can complete on their own.

A good rule of thumb: sub plans should be meaningful enough to support what you're teaching, but not so essential that you'll have to reteach everything if students don't do it.

For emergency sub plans, find something simple from one of the sources above, drop it in your folder, and turn it in. If you're ever in a situation where you truly need those emergency plans—say, something tragic has happened—the last thing you'll want to worry about is whether your students got a meaningful lesson that day.

When It All Goes to Crap

Even the best lessons fail. Sometimes the students aren't feeling it, and sometimes we're off our game.

Lessons fail for so many reasons—maybe the material was outside the *Zone of Proximal Development* for the students, meaning it was too hard or required too much heavy lifting for them (Vygotsky, 1978). Maybe the students weren't feeling it that day, and you need to work on building stronger relationships. There are hundreds of reasons a lesson could flop, and it really is a Murphy's Law situation, as I said before.

That being said, don't stress it. It is one lesson out of 180 you will teach that year, and the thousands of lessons you will teach over the course of a career. When lessons fail, we have such great opportunities for growth and to learn. Reflect on what went wrong. Identify the pain points that prevented the lesson from landing and make revisions for the next class or next year.

> When lessons fail, we have such great opportunities for growth and to learn.

Teaching a lesson you wrote is like playing a song you wrote. No one listening is going to know if you played the wrong note. So don't sweat it.

If you start each day knowing that your lesson *can* bomb, you'll be much less devastated when it does. And learning from our mistakes is how we can come back and suck a little less tomorrow.

Chapter Recap

- Great teaching can come from anywhere, so don't limit yourself and try new things.
- Standards are the roadmaps that help us find what we're teaching.
- Instruction naturally flows from teacher-centered to student-focused as we pass more ownership of learning to students.
- Don't plan for every minute! Leave time for wonder, and mishaps!
- No need to reinvent the wheel. Use the resources that are out there to find lessons and lesson ideas.
- When it all goes belly up, stay calm. It's only one lesson.

References

Anderson, L. W., & Krathwohl, D. R. (Eds.). (2001). *A taxonomy for learning, teaching, and assessing: A revision of Bloom's taxonomy of educational objectives.* Longman.

Bloom, B. S., Engelhart, M. D., Furst, E. J., Hill, W. H., & Krathwohl, D. R. (1956). *Taxonomy of educational objectives: The classification of educational goals. Handbook I: Cognitive domain.* Longmans, Green.

Common Core State Standards Initiative. (2010). *English language arts standards: Language. Grade 5.* National Governors Association Center for Best Practices & Council of Chief State School Officers. www.corestandards.org/ELA-Literacy/L/5/4/

Fisher, D., & Frey, N. (2008). *Better learning through structured teaching: A framework for the gradual release of responsibility.* ASCD.

Hammond, Z. (2015). *Culturally responsive teaching and the brain: Promoting authentic engagement and rigor among culturally and linguistically diverse students*. Corwin.

Loewen, J. W. (2007). *Lies my teacher told me: Everything your American history textbook got wrong* (Rev. ed.). The New Press.

Pashler, H., McDaniel, M., Rohrer, D., & Bjork, R. (2008). Learning styles: Concepts and evidence. *Psychological Science in the Public Interest, 9*(3), 105–119. https://doi.org/10.1111/j.1539-6053.2009.01038.x

Vygotsky, L. S. (1978). *Mind in society: The development of higher psychological processes*. Harvard University Press.

Willingham, D. T. (2009). *Why don't students like school? A cognitive scientist answers questions about how the mind works and what it means for the classroom*. Jossey-Bass.

3

Suck Less at Classroom Management: Control What You Can, Ignore What You Can't

The Day My Career Flashed before My Eyes

I remember it very clearly. Though it was nearly 20 years ago, the image is burned into my memory: a piece of a meter stick hurling through the air above my students' heads.

It was my first-year teaching, and I had completely lost control of the class. In a moment of frustration, I slammed the meter stick down on a table, hoping to scare the students into silence. Instead, a piece snapped off and sailed across the room. All I could think was, "This is how my career ends."

Luckily, the stick didn't hit anyone, and I didn't lose my job. But if my principal had walked by at that exact moment, I can't imagine what they would have thought.

I was out of control, but only because I had no control. I couldn't get the class to pay attention. I was constantly putting out fires. I'd go to one group to get them to stop talking, and they'd immediately point fingers: "But they're talking!" I'd end up going from talker to talker with the same results. It was endless. And I was at my wits' end.

Luckily, I've come a long way since my first-year teaching and learned a lot along the way. I've put in the work to manage my room and came out the other side.

Two Truths and No Lie

If you've ever struggled in the classroom or wondered why students won't "just behave." I have some news for you.

Before we begin, we have to agree on two truths.

First: You can't *make* anyone do anything in a classroom. You don't *make* students read. You can't *make* them sit still or be quiet. You are fundamentally unable to *make* students do anything.

Second: The only person in the classroom you can control is *you*. That's it. Just you.

So, what now?

If we can't force students to behave, listen, or learn, then we have to get them to *want* to do those things. What that means is, classroom management is manipulation. That is how we're going to get students to do what we need them to do.

That's not a bad thing. All classroom management is manipulation. You're persuading, nudging, and incentivizing. You're convincing students to read, take notes, pay attention, follow directions, or whatever else you have planned for the day.

> If we can't force students to behave, listen, or learn, then we have to get them to *want* to do those things.

This doesn't mean you need to be Machiavellian about it. It's not coercion, it's persuasion.

Think back to your favorite teachers, I'm sure it wasn't the ones that were so strict or scary you didn't dare to step out of line. It was probably also not the classes that had no structure, where you could do whatever you wanted. Likely, it was the one where you felt compelled to behave and actually learned stuff.

Why were you compelled to behave? Probably because they took the steps to make you *want* to behave.

The good news? You *can* get better. Classroom management is a skill. It's learnable. You can build the kind of class culture you've always wanted, but it's going to take work. Which I know can sound frustrating. But if you're going to teach them, you're going to have to learn how to manage them first.

Everyone struggles with classroom management. Everyone. From veterans to newbies, no one has a perfect class each day. It's learning the teacher moves that will someday be automatic that helps you manage the classroom. It's learning what to overlook, learning when to be firm, and knowing yourself and your boundaries.

Yes, it is exhausting, but at the end of the day, you're doing all this so you can teach your freaking lesson.

No Substitute for a Well-Planned Lesson

When it comes to managing student behavior, there is no substitute for a well-planned lesson. When your lesson is on point, students will fall in line much more quickly. It's the days when you haven't had much time to plan, you're winging it, or something has gone wrong that the students will get out of line. Trust me. When you have each step down and are laser-focused on what to do next, it'll go a long way to making your classroom much more well-behaved.

Don't Smile until December

You've maybe heard expressions like "warm demander" or "no-nonsense nurturer." What they're all getting at is the same idea: be firm but fair. Set boundaries early.

When people say "don't smile until December," they don't mean to be cold or robotic. They mean: start firm, and loosen up as you build relationships. If you begin the year being permissive—about seating charts, phones, talking, eating, whatever—it's going to be a lot harder to rein things in later. It's not easy to put the toothpaste back in the tube.

But smile on day one if you want to.

Classroom Management Starts at the Door

Classroom management doesn't begin when the bell rings and class starts. Managing your class starts as students enter your room.

So many issues can be prevented by standing at your door and greeting. Standing at the door is a good way to direct students to what they need to get started on, check for uniforms or dress code, remind students to put their phones away, but most importantly, it's a vibe check for your students.

While standing at the door, you can high five, fist bump, and greet each student. This allows you to set the tone as friendly and familiar, and check for any issues students might be having. Put on your empathy hat as you look for students who are upset, bummed out, tired, or overly excited. Get a feel for what they are feeling and take steps to make sure you're ready for what they are bringing to the classroom energy.

If I have a clearly distressed student, I'll pull them aside and check in with them. Even if they don't want to tell me or talk about it, just them knowing I noticed and care will go a long way.

Standing at the door also allows students to greet you. Ninety-nine percent of the time, it'll be to ask, "Are we doing anything today?" But sometimes it can be for a more serious issue or logistical situation, like being picked up before the end of the period.

If you're a teacher who has your students all day, such as an elementary teacher, greeting your students is even more crucial because you're setting the tone for the next six hours.

There are videos out there of teachers who greet each student with a special handshake and greeting. Get into it. Do what works for you at the end of the day, but there is no limit to how you greet them.

A lot can be gleaned by standing at your door, and it's a great habit to get into. So, get out there and greet those students!

One Word: Seating Chart

If I had a dollar for every time a teacher told me their class was out of control and they didn't have a seating chart, I'd have a crap ton of dollars. Seriously. You can't expect a quiet(er) classroom if you're not telling kids where to sit, providing structure, or laying a foundation.

While it is true that I taught an AP class for years and would often not give those classes a seating chart, those classes were smaller and self-selected by students who wanted the challenge.

But chances are, you're going to want a seating chart.

A seating chart lets you separate friends without making a scene. It lets you separate enemies, too. It quietly says, *I'm in charge* and reminds students that there is some structure in your classroom. It's a small move with big results.

No Shame in the Row Game

If you have a particularly rowdy bunch of students or are still figuring out your management style, nothing is better than old-fashioned rows. Rows allow you to minimize talking, simply because there is more space, and also allow you to maximize the distance between talkative students.

While rows have gotten a bad rap in these days of group learning and cooperative teams, at the end of the day, you need to be able to teach, and if you can't teach because there is too much talking, rows are the solution to that problem. For Pete's sake, do rows.

On the first day of class, I always start with rows. You don't know who your talkers are yet, and you don't want to have to change the seating chart on day two. The best thing to do, though, is just to sit alphabetically so you can learn their names quickly as well.

There will be students who are used to sitting by their neighbors, and you will get some talking; this is okay. These first three weeks, think of yourself as an investigator. You're figuring out who your quiet and not-so-quiet students are. I always lie and tell the students we'll be in rows until I learn everyone's names, the truth is we stay in rows until I learn everyone's habits, establish our classroom norms (like the quiet signal, more on that later), and I have collected enough formative data to make an informed seating chart, which is usually about three weeks.

Ideally, you'll get the hang of things with rows, which will lead you to be able to do whatever kind of classroom formation that suits your style, if that's what you want.

Other Setups

Besides rows, you can put students in pairs, that are still rows, that is, two desks together, but in rows. This allows you to use some grouping techniques, like a "turn and talk," but still minimize the overall distractions and talking that groups can promote. This also allows you to create strategic pairs as well.

Strategic Pairings

Use your quiet students to your advantage. Got a talkative student? Surround them with your quiet students, opposite sex, or introverts.

By mid-year, you should have a good idea of who would work well together and who would not. And you should be able to reward those students who have earned it by sitting with a friend, and still keep certain students isolated from one another.

You can seat kids next to people who:

- Are *slightly* more focused
- Are *quiet leaders*
- Will nudge them without enabling bad behavior.

Teams or Groups

And then lastly, there are pods, or groups of three to five, depending on how many students you have. Ideally, you'd make groups of four. This is a popular way to seat students nowadays as it leads to more interaction and teamwork.

Homogeneous vs. Heterogeneous Grouping

Whether you call them table groups, pods, or teams, arranging students into small groups is a common classroom strategy. Before creating those groups, though, you'll need to consider an important question: Should your groups be *homogeneous* (students with similar characteristics) or *heterogeneous* (students with diverse characteristics)?

There are times when homogeneous groups make sense. For example, if you're grouping students by reading level, or maybe English learners to provide targeted language support, or balancing out a heavily skewed gender ratio, you might choose to group students who share certain traits. These decisions should be based on the needs of your students and your goals for instruction.

However, a significant body of research suggests that heterogeneous groups are generally more effective for promoting cooperation, social connection, and academic growth. Studies, such as those by educational researcher Spencer Kagan, have shown that students in diverse groups are more likely to form friendships across ethnic and cultural lines and often experience better overall learning outcomes (Kagan, 1999).

The way I create heterogeneous groups is usually based on some measure of ability. This is how Kagan Cooperative Learning does it. Personally, I use recent test scores, reading level, or overall grade in the class to group them. I try to get a high flyer, a medium flyer, a low hanger, and a low performer and put them together. This allows students to be challenged by those they sit with but also to have some comfort as well. If you constantly put your struggling students together, you're in for a group that will get off task or fall behind.

Creating Heterogeneous Groups

One simple way to think about building heterogeneous groups is to ensure a balance across key identifiers. Consider the following when creating your teams:

- Gender identity
- Ethnic and cultural background

- Language proficiency
- Academic strengths
- Social dynamics

By intentionally creating diverse groups, you help foster a classroom where students build empathy, challenge assumptions, and learn from each other's experiences.

Groups facilitate talking. If you're not going to have your students talking regularly, through turn-and-talks or some other structure, then don't put them in groups. Groups are designed for students to be able to talk, support each other, and if that isn't what you're going for, you should keep them apart.

Sharing Rooms

The reality today is that many teachers are forced to share classrooms with other teachers. If you're a novice teacher, you might not have the clout to dictate the way the room is laid out. Maybe you want rows, but the teacher you share with swears on teams. In that case, remember what I said above and put the time and effort into a well-thought-out seating chart. You can't control everything, but you can always control your seating chart.

Changing the Seating Chart Regularly

The seating chart is not immutable. The seating chart should serve the needs of your classroom and promote student learning. Change it when you need to. Move students when you need to.

Students will adapt to a new seating chart and make new friends, which is good. We want them to have a diverse group of friends, but that means they'll start to talk again after you create a new seating chart. You'll want to rotate it every nine weeks or so at a minimum, but in reality, it can be as often as you need to do it.

A new seating chart can also be a "soft reset" after a break or long weekend. It can be a good way to reset the classroom and reset expectations as needed. Remember, you don't owe it to students to let them sit where they want; it's your classroom, so put them where it makes sense for you.

Seating charts aren't marriage certificates. They're just scaffolding. Tear them down and rebuild as needed.

Emergency Moves

What to Do If a Seating Chart Still Blows Up?

- **Mini-moves:** Move a couple of students or have them swap places. You can't know how your seating chart will play out in real life, so it's okay if you have to tweak it sometimes.
- **Group Swaps:** I keep my students in groups, but sometimes I have to move my back groups to the front, etc.

A Quiet Signal

I can't stress this enough: get yourself a quiet signal. I didn't have one in my first couple of years teaching, and I would *never* go back. You've got to have a plan. If you don't have a plan to get students quiet, what are you left with? Talking over them? Shouting? Flashing the lights or worse yet, the sarcastic "I'll wait?" They probably never covered this in your teacher prep program, I know mine didn't, but you need to have a way to get the students quiet while keeping your cool and also making sure everyone, including you, is being respectful.

I've seen a ton of different quiet signals over the years. One teacher rang a hotel bell, another shook a little sleigh bell, and one used a Tibetan singing bowl. There are *so* many things you can do. What matters is that it's consistent and you stick with it.

A quiet signal is respectful. Think about what a teacher means when they say "I'll wait." What they're actually saying is "shut up." Because if they were going to wait, they'd just stand there and wait, no need to announce it like someone posting they're "taking a break from social media." That announcement is just a polite way of saying "quiet down," and students know it.

My Quiet Signal

My signal is simple, and I totally stole it from Kagan Cooperative Learning. I raise my hand in the air and say, "Signal, please." Then I wait. That's it. Sometimes I'll add a little countdown, but if I do, I always keep it light. I'll say something like, "Do you know what happens when I get to zero? If I get to zero and you're still talking, I'll count down again. Don't believe me? I'll count down so many times."

The point is, I'm never yelling at my students to get quiet. Here's how I introduce it:

There will be times when I need you to get quiet. I could flash the lights, or say, 'I'll wait,' or go 'shhh' at you—but I won't. Instead, I'll raise my hand and say, 'Signal please.' I say *please* because I respect you, and I hope you'll respect me. When I raise my hand, three things happen:

1. You stop what you're doing,
2. You focus on me,
3. You raise your hand in the air to signal others.

It's very simple: my hand goes up; your hand goes up. My hand goes up, your hand goes up.

(As I say this, I alternate raising my hands to show the pattern.)

Then we practiced it. I say, "Talk to your neighbor for a bit—I'm going to bring us back with the signal. You won't know when it's coming, so be ready."

After a minute or so, I use the signal, praise the students, and keep moving. Easy.

The key is: you can't biff the signal. You *have* to own it. If you hesitate or look unsure, students will pick up on it and ignore it. Honestly, that's true for every quiet signal I've ever seen—You. Have. To. Own. It.

Other Quiet Signals I've Seen

- "Clap once (or twice) if you can hear my voice."
  - Or pointing ("Point up if you can hear me. Now point left," etc.)
- Call and response (e.g., "Class class!" → "Yes, yes!")
  - "Red Robin!" → "Yummm" (Yes, this was a second-grade classroom.)
- Bells & Whistles
- Flashing the lights
- "1,2,3 eyes on me"
- A rain stick.

In the end, it's not about which one you pick—it's about finding one that *you* can use consistently and confidently.

No one enjoys raising their voice to get students' attention. Hopefully, with a quiet signal, those moments will be few and far between.

At this point, you might be thinking, "I don't need a quiet signal." I used to feel that same way, but let's do some math here.

If it takes you one minute to get your students quiet each day, just one single minute, that is 180 minutes a year. That's anywhere from two to four entire class periods of time. Think about that.

Imagine that it's back-to-school night and you're talking with some parents, only to say,

> I'm very excited to teach your students this year. But I will spend 4 class periods trying to get the class quiet. I know you expect me to teach them for 180 days, but four of them will be spent on me trying to get them calmed down.

And that is only if it takes you one minute a day.

How many times in a period might you have to get your students quiet? How many minutes? How many class periods will you spend trying to get their attention?

If you're teaching at a school with less than an hour periods, and you're spending up to five minutes a day every time you need the class to calm down, you're losing almost two weeks of instruction. Not due to poor planning. Not due to bad behavior. Simply for lack of a routine.

I know a quiet signal can seem elementary, but trust me when I say it is worth it.

I use my quiet signal with 9th grade to 12th, and primarily 12th grade. You can do it too. I believe in you.

Calling Home

Call home as often as your schedule allows. Some years, for me, that's 10 times, sometimes it's 50 times, it really depends on how the year is going and how overwhelmed I'm feeling.

At the end of the day, the front office and admin should be the point of contact for attendance and behavior issues, so if you're not able to call for that, don't sweat it.

So, when should you call home? There are two types of calls you can make: either a positive call home (and students, of course, love these, and so do parents) or a negative call home. I try and call home as often as I can for positive calls and only do a negative call when needed.

The Positive Call Home

Something I like to do is give a positive phone call home for students on Fridays. Sometimes I'll do it in class, right in front of kids (during that 5% buffer time) and let parents know how great their student is right then and there.

You'd be surprised how a positive call home can diffuse tension with students and let them know you care. And at the risk of sounding like a cliché, students knowing that you care is all they care about.

I say something simple when I call, which goes a little like this:

> Is this so-and-so's parent? Hi, this is Mr. Glassford. I just wanted to call and tell you how great your student has been in class. They've been crushing it with their assignments and participation.

They will usually say something about how great it is to get a phone call like this, and then I end with:

> Just wanted to share that with you—hope you have a fantastic day.

That's it. Sweet and simple.

The Negative Call Home

Any time I send a student out of my room, I call home. Period.

If a student acts in a way that means they need to miss out on learning, then I make it a point to call home for two reasons: first, you can't always count on the office to follow up with a phone call, and second, we should hope that parents are helping to reinforce positive behavior in the classroom.

I call home during my planning period or in the moment, so I don't forget.

For a student who is consistently disruptive, I also like to call home on Fridays if their behavior hasn't improved. That way, it's more likely the message sticks, and the behavior doesn't carry over into the next week.

When I do need to make a negative call home, I keep it short and factual. I avoid emotional language or assigning intent. For example:

> Hello, is this so-and-so's parent? This is Mr. Glassford, their teacher. Today in class, we had an issue. Your student told

me to 'get off his d***' while I was redirecting him, and I had to remove him from class. I was hoping you could speak with him about appropriate language in the classroom.
(Based on a true story)

Usually, the parent will respond with concern or an apology.

I then thank them for their time and move on. It doesn't help to dwell. If you dwell, you risk saying something you might regret or getting into picking sides or something. Your best bet is to just call, state the behavior, and get off the phone.

When to Remove Students

If it isn't a violation of the respectful nature in the classroom, then I don't send students out. Students are young, and their brains are still developing; they're going to make mistakes. Anything I can deal with in-house, I will. As one teacher told me, sometimes you just have to "close your door and teach," meaning that at the end of the day, what happens in your room is on you, and you should try to deal with what you can.

If you try to micromanage every behavior and wait until all students are sitting perfectly still and silent before teaching, you'll never get to your lesson.

So, I only kick kids out for the big stuff: disrespect to a person in a way that violates their dignity, such as bullying or hate speech, or completely disrespecting me, such as the above scenario.

A Note on Removing Students

Once you've removed a student from class, let it go.

I always say, "See you tomorrow," as they leave, so they know I'm not mad at them. Their brains are still developing, and it's our job, as the adults in the room, to model emotional regulation and not hold grudges. Holding onto that tension? That's a recipe for an ulcer.

> When you kick a student out, that's where it should end—you've already won. I once watched a teacher remove a student and then keep yelling at them to "get out" and "move faster." If you've already embarrassed a student in front of their peers, be prepared for them to push back. They're trying to save face.
>
> Remember, kicking students out is easy. Keeping them in the room and figuring out how to deal with the issue is hard. It can become very enticing to just boot students the moment they act up and get them out of your hair. I get it. I do.
>
> In my first-year teaching I kicked out 90 students in 90 days, maybe more. There wasn't a single teacher in the building who kicked out more students than me, and I'll tell you I learned about as much as the students I kicked out did, which wasn't very much. Figuring out how to solve your problems in-house will go a lot further in your journey to mastering classroom management.

Ignore What You Can

On one teaching rubric I've experienced for evaluating teacher lessons, there's a section on managing student behavior. To earn the highest scores, you must "ignore inconsequential behavior." Think about that, to earn the highest score you must allow some misbehavior to go uncorrected. What? If you spend all your time putting out every fire you'll never get to the lesson. You have to learn which hills to die on and which aren't worth the fight. Maybe a student is "secretly" reading a book in their lap, but still taking some notes. Or maybe a student was quietly chatting with their neighbor for a second during a transition. It can be anything, but if it isn't disrupting the flow of the lesson, it is best to leave these things unchecked.

Some teaching books and philosophies say "100% of students, 100% of the time," but I'm here to tell you that you just need 90% of students, 90% of the time.

What does that mean?

> As long as all your students get almost all of your lessons, you're doing alright.

It means as long as all your students get almost all of your lessons, you're doing alright. Students are going to get distracted. They're going to talk to their friends, they're going to doodle, or work on other class assignments during your class time. It's going to happen.

Nobody is perfect at classroom management, and trying to be is going to drive you crazy. Meet the students where they are. Some students will be engaged at different times and with different things.

This doesn't mean we give up on students or let some fall through the cracks; it means we just accept that today, very few students have the attention span to sit through a 90-minute class, and maybe we lose some for periods of time.

But as long as the students are mostly picking up most of what you're laying down, you're doing fine.

Setting Yourself Up for Success

In their book, *Switch* by Chip and Dan Heath talk about how in each of us there is an elephant (our emotional side), a rider (or logical side), and the path (the way we do things) (Heath & Heath, 2010). The path is the thing we change when we want to make it easier on the elephant to get in line, but not sure if the rider can handle it. Meaning, students are going to be emotional and make bad decisions. I know I've said this already, but it is worth repeating: their brains are still developing, they just aren't able to make the decisions that are always in their best interest. So, what do we do? We make it easier for them to find their way to where we want them to go. Meet their needs before they become a problem.

You need to design your classroom to be the path for students. Make it easy for them to behave.

Here are some things I do to make the path smoother for my students and help them feel comfortable:

- ♦ Using lamps instead of overhead lights to make my room more relaxed.

- Set up a "book nook" with a rug, pillows, and throw blankets (for when the room is too cold).
- Use an essential oil diffuser to make the room smell nice.
- Bring in plants—according to Badali (2025), Herrmann and Evans' study at Weber State found that placing plants in classrooms was associated with higher student grades (Badali, 2025).
- Hang posters and pictures that reflect my personality and make the room more fun (do not let your room look like an operating room. Hang some things on the wall!).
- Created a "student use section" with lotion, hand sanitizer, tissues, extra pencils, stapler, three-hole punch, etc., an area that says "I'm meeting your needs."

You need to do what fits your school, your budget, and your style. Not all schools are okay with students using blankets, and some won't let you plug in small electronics, but at the end of the day, the more you can do to make your classroom a place students want to be, the more likely you are to have students who want to be there.

Motivating Students

We would all love for our students to be motivated to learn intrinsically. But the truth is, students aren't, and they don't want to be at school most of the time. Sometimes all you have are carrots and sticks.

I have taken to giving away trophies in my classroom. I order a box of tiny trophies and medals and give them out for things like perfect scores on tests, high scores in games, and winning in class challenges.

Also, most students are surprisingly food motivated, and yes, we have to worry about allergies these days, but a little candy will go a long way.

Praise, Praise, Praise

Praise can work wonders with your students. If you've ever read *How Full Is Your Bucket?* (Clifton & Rath, 2004), you'd see that the more confident and "full" we are on praise, the more likely we are to "fill other people's buckets." If you take some time to build up your students, you'd be surprised at how well they can pay it forward.

"Catch them being good," as the saying goes. I try to dole out as many "great jobs" as possible when students do anything in the classroom. High fives, fist bumps, and "atta boys" will take you far.

When students are "full," they are less likely to misbehave and more likely to "fill up" a classmate. I literally used to have a spot on my lesson plan that said "buckets" for me to check off to make sure I filled buckets each class period. Praise is the gift that keeps on giving.

Digital Carrots and Sticks

One common tool in the classroom behavior toolkit is *Class Dojo*, a platform that automates a classic "carrot and stick" approach—rewarding positive behaviors and discouraging negative ones. Teachers can assign points for actions like helping a peer (+2) or subtract points for things like being on a phone without permission (−3). It's also an easy way to keep a running log of student behaviors and patterns throughout the day.

What's more, *Class Dojo* allows families to view their student's point totals in real time, which builds a bridge between classroom conduct and home conversations.

Here's how I use it: each week, I call home to celebrate the student with the highest point total. It's a simple, positive contact—and after the call, I reset their points to make space for someone else the following week.

Is it the perfect way to motivate students? Not even close. But it's simple, and students respond well to it if you use it consistently.

On Choices and Manipulation

As stated previously, classroom management is a form of manipulation. In *Teaching with Love and Logic* (Fay & Funk, 1995), they state that students want control, and you can either give it to them on your terms or they'll take it on theirs. Honestly, who am I kidding? We all want control. The trick is recognizing your own need for control, coming to terms with it, and then intentionally offering your students small but meaningful choices.

Think about how little control students actually have in their lives. Depending on the school and subject, they may be told what classes to take, where to sit, what to wear, when to arrive, when to leave, what they can eat, when they can or can't use their phones, and when they're allowed to go to the bathroom. In this age of standardized testing and teaching to the test, students are micromanaged more than ever and given very little autonomy.

So, of course, students are going to be on edge. According to a study by Baumeister, Bratslavsky, Muraven, and Tice (1998), self-control is a finite resource. Meaning, we can deplete our self-control, and when we do, making tough decisions becomes even harder. Students are immediately using theirs as soon as they enter the building. Phones are away, they are doing challenging work, etc. We would all rather play on our devices or stream videos, but we've got work to do.

Giving students choices is like giving them a little more rope to work with. It lets them reclaim a bit of autonomy, which helps restore their self-control. And it helps you relax, too, because when they *think* they're in charge, you don't have to fight for it constantly.

There are a million ways you can give up some control, but I have some "go-tos" when it comes to giving up just the right amount of power.

The first is simple: lighting. I have the overhead lights on when students enter the room, and then I ask, "Do you want the lights off?" They always say yes, and I'm totally fine with that because I have plenty of lamps around the room. It costs me nothing, but they feel like they've had a say. That little moment sets a tone: this classroom is a shared space.

My second favorite tactic is what I call the "due date trick." When I'm assigning work, I'll ask, "Do you want this due on Thursday or Friday?" They almost always pick Friday, which is great, because I was going to have it due Friday anyway. You can do variations on this, like: "Turn it in at the end of class or the start of class tomorrow?" Either way, they're doing what I planned, but they feel like they made the call.

These moments build trust, which feels bad maybe since we're kind of tricking them, but students begin to see you as someone who respects their autonomy. And the more they feel that, the more likely they are to meet you halfway on the stuff that really matters. You "give up" a little control, but what you get back is a more collaborative, respectful classroom culture.

Recently, in the classroom, I created the illusion of control for my students and gave one of them a big win.

STUDENT: I will pay you $20 if we don't have to take our quiz today.
ME: Ha ha, I can't take your money.
STUDENT: Okay, play me in Rock, Paper, Scissors then!
ME: Okay, let's play.

He beats me. Twice.

ME TO THE CLASS: Well, everyone, due to recent events, I guess we're not taking the quiz today.

Big cheers all around. The student looked like a hero. It was great. Because here's the thing, I had already decided not to give them the quiz that day anyway. Did they know that? No. Did I ever tell them? No. But that student will likely be telling the story of this day for years to come.

Other examples of "choices" I've used with students:

- ♦ The "Vote" on Next Activity
  - You give students a choice between two things you've already planned, and would be fine doing either way. They feel empowered. You get buy-in.

- The "Do You Want 5 More Minutes or 10?" Timer Extension
  - Wait until you've got about ten minutes left for students to work, and then ask the class this question. Again, you were going to give them the ten anyway. The best part is you can add something like "okay, we'll go 10 more minutes, but everyone better make sure to finish." Classic.
- Silent Choice in Reading or Writing Prompts
  - Offering multiple writing prompts or reading options makes them feel in control of their learning, though you know they all lead to the same skill objective.
- Read aloud or by yourself
  - Both get the text read, but you give them a choice on how to do it.
- Do you want me to pick your groups, or do you want to pick your groups?
  - Only do this one if you truly don't care who they work with because they're picking their groups here.

Placebo Buttons, or the Illusion of Control

In a 2018 article by CNN (Prisco, 2018), they exposed the existence of "placebo buttons." If you're as confused as I was when I read this article, placebo buttons are buttons that exist in the world that don't do anything. Well, that's not true; they do something, but what they do is give the illusion of control. So, for example, the walk buttons at some crosswalks don't actually do anything. So why do they exist? Because if you press the button, you're more likely to stand and wait for the signal to change, as you believe you have some control over it. Another popular button is the "door close" button on elevators. Since the passing of the Americans with Disabilities Act, elevators have a set time they must stay open, which doesn't keep some people from spamming the button, thinking they're keeping someone out or shortening their ride.

What's my point? My point is, placebo buttons work. They create compliance, they give a semblance of control where none exists, and they help make people behave in ways that are beneficial to society. What are your placebo buttons? What can you do in the classroom that gives the illusion of control and helps you maintain the environment you want?

> **Speaking of Placebos**
>
> Back in 1961, Stanley Milgram conducted his now-infamous experiment in which participants believed they were administering harmful, electric shocks to another participant. What the Milgram Experiment tells us is that around 65% of people respond to figures of authority (Milgram, 1963). This is why I wear a tie to work. People have been socialized to treat people dressed up a certain way.
>
> My thought is that the tie is the classroom equivalent of the lab coat. I have noticed that when I wear a tie, and even sometimes a suit, the students are better behaved. If students have been socialized to associate professional dress with authority, why not lean into that and make it work in our favor? People have been socialized to treat people dressed up in a certain way. I say use that knowledge and give yourself an edge in a classroom.

> **Putting on the Uniform**
>
> Another thing that dressing up does for me, personally, is that it allows me to disassociate the student behavior from myself. When I dress up, I am "Mr. Glassford." Whatever happened at work that day, whatever students did or said, whatever problems that arose, those are "Mr. Glassford's" problems. When I get home and shed my uniform, costume, or cosplay (whatever you want to call it), I become Carlton again. When I'm Carlton, it is easier to separate myself from Mr. Glassford. It helps me remember that students aren't talking to me personally but are talking to this teacher persona I have created for school.

> I'm not all authoritative with my dress. I wear a bowtie on Wednesdays (for bowtie Wednesday), and I do "Fun Tie Thursday," in which I wear a fun printed tie (I also do "no tie-day Friday," I'm not a complete stick-in-the-mud. I do still have fun). I just set clear boundaries with myself mentally that say "this is teacher me" and when I'm home, "this is real me," and that allows me to have a little more work-life balance.
>
> If you're able to do so, I recommend setting up a different attire than you normally wear. If you find yourself too relaxed when wearing jeans, maybe consider something a bit more formal.

Consequences as Choices

There are a variety of ways you can dole out consequences to students, but I'm going to share my favorite way to redirect behaviors I don't want in the classroom. *Language of Choice* from *Win-Win Discipline* (Kagan, 2001) is my go-to. The way it works, summarizing here, is to offer two choices to the students, where one is a natural consequence, and one is a responsible choice.

"The responsible thing to do is to keep your hands to yourself. If you can't keep your hands to yourself, you'll have to move seats." If they continue to misbehave, you would say something like, "It is evident by your behavior that you are choosing to move seats, is that correct?"

Another way I use it is to take students out in the hall and talk about their misbehavior. I rarely lecture as no student has ever sat through a teacher's lecture and been like "they are so right, I will *totally* change my behavior. This *is* important to my future." That's not what is going through the mind of any student, regardless of their age. Anyway, I take them to the hall, and I say, "You can either (whatever it is I need them to do), or you can choose to go to the office. The choice is yours. I'm sure you'll choose the responsible thing," and then I walk back in the room and leave them in the hall. They have never chosen to go to the office.

The heart of the structure is to give two choices, both of which you're okay with, and let the student choose to come back, participate, or get it together. When that doesn't work, you move to the "you're choosing to go to the office, then? Is that correct?" Or whatever your consequence may be.

Natural Consequences

I'm not a big fan of punishing students. It's not that I think students should avoid consequences; it's that the goal should never be punishment. If you're calling home, writing a referral, or sending a kid out just to get back at them, you've already lost the plot.

There should be consequences for student actions. That's not what I'm saying. But the consequences should be natural and not personal. The natural consequence of cheating might be that you get a zero on the assignment. The natural consequence of disrespecting a student in a hateful way might be that you lose the privilege of being in class for the day. Regardless, it's not personal; it's the natural consequence. If a student abuses the bathroom pass, the natural consequence might be needing to stay in class unless there's a medical need.

One trick I've found surprisingly effective is simply asking, "Can you wait a few minutes?" A lot of the time, they'll sit back down and forget they even had to go. It gives them a moment to reflect, and it gives you the opportunity to redirect without saying no outright. Try it. It works more often than you'd think.

Don't Take It Personal

Speaking of consequences, don't take it personally when students misbehave. I once knew a teacher who said on day one, a student walked in her room and said, "Oh great, another b****." What did she do? She said, "You've made your hypothesis, let's see if you're right by the end of the year." Why didn't she flip out? Why didn't she call the office and seek to ruin this student's day? Because she knew he was already having a bad day. This was less than one minute into class on the first day of school. Whatever this child was going through had nothing to do with her, and she knew it. Sure, she would have been within her rights to kick him out, but what would that have done? She didn't meet aggression with aggression. She responded with humor and humanity, and it completely disarmed him. He expected her to kick him out. He may have even wanted to get kicked out, but that wasn't what happened.

Here's the truth: most of the student misbehavior isn't about you. They likely have other things going on in their life. They might be hating school, which we've alluded to reasons why that is, that might be hating "teacher" (as a representative of said school), but they generally are not personally upset with you. Remember that they don't have fully developed brains yet, and you do, so you should be the one to keep your cool. You need to recognize misbehavior for what it is.

> ### Why Do Babies Cry?
>
> Babies cry because they have a need that isn't being met. They are wet, or tired, or hungry, or a million other things, but mostly they cry because they are unable to express their needs with words. All behavior is communication. Students misbehave because they are communicating their needs when they don't have the words. When a student throws something across the room they might be saying "I'm lost" or "I don't understand" when a student refuses to put away their cell phone, they might be saying "I'm upset and this is my comfort item" they could be saying any number of things but finding out where the behavior is coming from is part of the job.
>
> Next time a student acts up in class, instead of reacting to their behavior with a knee-jerk, ask yourself, "What is this student trying to tell me?" or "What need is not being met?" That's why I build my classroom environment with intention: calming music, soft lighting, an essential oil diffuser, and even snacks, because when students feel safe and seen, they act out less.

Rules

I'm not a big fan of "rules" per se, at least not at the micro level, but I have put a few in after the meter stick incident. Of course, I enforce all school policies when I am teaching because that's my job, but I try not to create too many rules in my classroom.

That isn't to say rules can't be effective. If it works for you, I'm not going to knock it. Instead, I create expectations that I want students to meet, and then I have procedures that we follow.

My concern is that if you have a rule for everything, students will begin finding ways to get around the rules or do something that is not in the rules. Did your rule say "no throwing pencils?" Well what if they throw around erasers? Is that breaking the rules? Did the rule say to stay in your seat? What if they scooch the seat across the room but without leaving it? Is that against the rules? It's much easier to set an overall expectation than it is to have an ever-growing list of rules.

Being Consistent

I cannot stress this enough: be consistent. If you enforce a rule on Monday, you had better enforce that rule on Tuesday. Students will pay attention to that and will push your buttons and your limits. This is something I struggled with when I first started teaching. I would let things slide because it was easier than fighting the same freaking fight day after day. It is exhausting.

But the truth is, you have got to do it. You need to find the resolve to be consistent. We've already spoken about how routine can create safety, and consistency can do the same, too.

I once had a couple of students who did not want to sit in their assigned seats. Every single day at the start of class, they would not be where they were supposed to be. I would politely ask them to go to their seats, and they would reluctantly go. But one day, I stopped asking, I got tired of fighting it, and before you knew it, I didn't have a seating chart anymore. It became a free-for-all with students sitting where they wanted because I had stopped telling these other students to go to their seats. And they'll make all kinds of arguments like "we're not talking" or "I work better by them," but at the end of the day, you gotta hold the line.

And what happened to me? Well, I ended up with a chaotic classroom where I had to put my foot down and pull out my seating chart, and make everyone return to where they were supposed to sit. The class got mad and acted like I was the jerk for enforcing my policy.

What should I have done? I should have taken the few students who kept not sitting in their seats to the hallway and had a conversation that looked like this.

> I know you don't want to sit in your seats, but I have created a seating chart that works for me and for this class period. If you have an issue with where you are sitting or can't see the board, you are more than welcome to email me about the issue. It is important that everyone follow the same expectations in the classroom. Is there any reason you are unable to sit where you are assigned?

Being consistent doesn't mean being mean. It means setting a norm and enforcing that norm to ensure that everyone knows what to expect. And, it'll pay dividends in the long run in reducing behavioral issues.

My One Expectation

"Be kind, courteous, and respectful at all times." That's it. That's my one expectation. It covers it all, but students still need things spelled out for them. Once I introduce my expectation, I give some examples of what that means. Not talking while I am, it's not respectful to do that. Not throwing things at people, that's not very kind. Saying "please" and "thank you" is a way of being courteous. It's all covered by this expectation. And I repeat it like a mantra, day in, day out, whenever a student violates the norm.

I simply ask them, "Was that kind, courteous, or respectful?" and they always know the answer.

The Lifeline that Is Procedures

As Harry Wong would say, you need procedures. A big reason my first year was so bad was because I didn't have any procedures. All I had was my one expectation and thought that would be enough for 13-year olds to handle. And oh, how wrong I was.

What I've learned is that in lieu of rules, you can have procedures for behavior that reinforce your values in the classroom. Procedures allow you to design your class the way you want to design it.

Sample Procedures:

- When to get out of your seat
- How to throw away trash
- How to ask to use the restroom
- How to use the pencil sharpener
- How to enter or exit the room.

If students have to do it, you can practice it, and they can learn it.

Classroom Management Frequently Encountered Issues

The following are a series of issues you may encounter in the classroom, and maybe you haven't thought out how you want to deal with them. I'll share what works for me and why I do it the way that I do.

Sleeping Students

If I'm being honest, I'm pretty loud when I'm teaching, so I don't get too many students putting their heads down, so tip one: use your teacher voice. But on occasion, I do get students who fall asleep in my class.

I try not to take it personally when a student falls asleep in class. You never know what their life is like or what their home situation is, so I try to respond with logic and not emotion.

The first thing I do is redirect the student. Which is like "no crap" because we're all going to do that, but the second thing I do is tell the student to go get a drink of water. By having them take a trip to the water fountain, I get the blood moving, get that oxygen and glucose going to the brain, and hopefully wake them up a little. It also says "I care" and "you can't sleep here" at the same time, which is nice.

An approach for me, which works at the high school level, is my "everyone gets one" rule. I give all of my students one day when they can disengage. That doesn't mean I let them use their phone or play games on their computer. Occasionally, you will have a student who just can't keep their head up. Maybe they didn't sleep last night, maybe they don't feel well, but parents won't come get them (or can't come get them), whatever it is, they just won't keep their head up. I wake them up for a brief second, and then I tell them, "Everyone gets one." That's me telling them they get one day; I'm going to leave them alone. Try to put your head down tomorrow, though, and we'll have issues.

If and/or when they come back the next day and try to put their head down, I remind them of our "deal," and that is usually enough to keep them up. If it isn't, we move to getting the water, and then escalate to a call home if they are unable to stay awake. In my nearly two decades of teaching, the "everyone gets one" has only come back for a round two a couple of times. For the most part, students respect my boundaries and are appreciative of my understanding approach.

Cellphones

We could probably write a book on cell phones in the classroom, and someone probably has. Here is what I have learned in my time: students will use the phones as much as you let them. It sucks having to police their behavior, but the truth is, if you start the year permissive with phones, you will have a phone problem all year. Start the year being strict on phones, and students will quickly learn that your class is not a class in which they can use phones.

Depending on your school policy and rules, you may be able to take phones away, or you might not. You'll need to set your threshold for technology in the classroom, but if I can issue a callback, this is one where you must stay consistent.

What Works for Me
Besides having a zero-tolerance policy on phones, my school has given everyone one of those hanging calculator holders for students to put their phones in at the start of class. If you're able to get the support of your administration, I recommend getting one. Hanging this thing up is one of the "paths" that I talked about earlier; it just makes it easier for students to give up their phones, especially if they see everyone else doing it.

Another thing I have seen teachers do, and this is school-dependent, is having students get "docked" if they get caught using their phones. For about 20 bucks online, you can get a multi-phone charging dock and use it to manage your classroom. If a student gets caught using their phone, they have to put it on the charger for the rest of the class. This is a less confrontational way of taking phones away, as most students will be a little more likely to give up their phone if they know it'll be full of juice to use in their next class.

Sometimes we have to get clever about how we get them to give up their phones, but you'll need to pick something because this issue is not going away.

Narrating When Things Go Well
So, this chapter focuses on what can go wrong, mostly, but things will go well. Hopefully, often. And when they do, make sure you highlight it. Let kids know you've caught them being good. Point it out. Shout it out. Thank them.

> Things will go well. Hopefully, often. And when they do, make sure you highlight it.

Squeezing in another technique, you can use this as an opportunity to narrate as well. Narrating is when you say things like "Jaden is ready to go," and "Aiden has his pencil out," or "Kaden is on task," and let the other students know that others are getting to it and they have permission to behave too. Permission is like what Malcolm Gladwell talks about in *The Tipping Point*, people subconsciously get "permission" from others to act a certain way (Gladwell, 2000). So, if you can highlight the good behavior, it'll let others know that it's okay to also behave.

Fountain of Youthful Distraction
You'd be surprised what a quick trip to the water fountain can solve. Have a student who's talking too much? Take a walk. Got a student who can't focus? Take a walk. Need to separate two students? Send one out to get a drink of water. When in doubt, a quick two-minute break to the water fountain can be your secret weapon.

If that doesn't work, and you have to get campus monitors, administrators, a dean, security, whatever your school has on duty, do so with grace and keep it about the behavior and not the student.

When You Lose Your Cool
While I hope this never happens to you, it might. There may come a day when you lose it on a student. I remember regrettably, a day I said something mean to a student after I was kicking them out. Not my best moment. But it happened.

What you do after you lose your cool is what is going to make or break you. Students know when they have pushed us too far, but that doesn't make it okay to snap. They deserve to feel safe at school.

So, when this does happen, you apologize. No need to grovel or make it a big show, but own up to it. Simply let them know, "I lost my cool. That wasn't okay. I'm sorry." That will go a long way to repairing the relationship and helping your class move on.

Final Thoughts
Classroom management isn't about being perfect. At the end of the day, it's about being intentional. It's about showing up for your students and creating a learning environment they can thrive in.

You don't have to be a master manipulator or the strictest teacher on the planet. You just have to keep trying. You will mess things up. You will lose your cool. You might even create a seating chart (or two) that blows up in your face. If you care enough to keep trying, your students will notice. So, take what works, toss out what doesn't, and come back tomorrow ready to suck a little less.

Chapter Recap

- You can only control yourself.
- Focus on procedures over rules.
- Use a quiet signal.
- Seating charts, seating charts, seating charts.
- Placebos are everywhere. Use them.
- Create an inviting environment.
- Consistency is key.
- Communicate with home for negative and positive.
- Ignore what you can.
- Take it one day at a time.

References

Badali, R. (2025, June 25). Weber State researchers find growth in student success by adding plants to classrooms. *WSU Today*. Weber State University. https://www.weber.edu/WSUToday/062525-plants-in-classrooms.html

Baumeister, R. F., Bratslavsky, E., Muraven, M., & Tice, D. M. (1998). Ego depletion: Is the active self a limited resource? *Journal of Personality and Social Psychology, 74*(5), 1252–1265. https://doi.org/10.1037/0022-3514.74.5.1252

Clifton, D. O., & Rath, T. (2004). *How full is your bucket? Positive strategies for work and life*. New York, NY: Gallup Press.

Fay, J., & Funk, D. (1995). *Teaching with love and logic: Taking control of the classroom*. Golden, CO: Love and Logic Press.

Gladwell, M. (2000). *The tipping point: How little things can make a big difference*. Boston, MA: Little, Brown and Company.

Heath, C., & Heath, D. (2010). *Switch: How to change things when change is hard*. Broadway Books.

Kagan, S. (1999, Winter). Cooperative learning: Seventeen pros and seventeen cons plus ten tips for success. *Kagan Online Magazine*. San Clemente, CA: Kagan Publishing. https://www.kaganonline.com

Kagan, S. (2001). *Win-win discipline: Strategies for all discipline problems*. Kagan Publishing.

Milgram, S. (1963). Behavioral study of obedience. *Journal of Abnormal and Social Psychology, 67*(4), 371–378. https://doi.org/10.1037/h0040525

Prisco, J. (2018, September 2). Illusion of control: Why the world is full of buttons that don't work. *CNN Style*. https://edition.cnn.com/style/article/placebo-buttons-design

4

Suck Less at Grading and Feedback: Tips and Tricks to Make Grading Sustainable

"I love grading!"—No teacher ever.

If I'm being honest, and who are we kidding, that seems to be my whole thing, grading is the worst part of teaching. Why can't we just give grades to students based on how much we like them? I kid, I kid.

All jokes aside, grading is not my strong suit. I've struggled with it and even resented it. What you're getting isn't some master plan from someone who has it all figured out—it's the stuff that's helped me survive, and make grading suck less.

Don't Grade Everything

This might feel obvious, but you don't have to grade everything ... though this won't stop students from asking, "Is this for a grade?"

A simple rule is "Don't grade anything you don't *have* to grade."

> Just because you pass it out doesn't mean they have to pass it back.

Ask yourself if the assignment is *practice* or *performance*. If it isn't demonstrating mastery, don't grade it. Mastery will vary based on the day's objective, but whatever mastery is, you're going to want to have a clear vision of it before you get started, and that will help to decide what to grade.

Remember, just because you pass it out doesn't mean they have to pass it back.

Mastery doesn't always show up in a worksheet or work sample, and instead, it's when a student is able to explain a concept to their neighbor better than I could. Mastery can take many forms, so be flexible with what you choose to grade.

Your school will, undoubtedly, have guidelines for how many and how often grades need to be updated. This will inform your practice, and might lead to you grading things you wish you didn't have to. Of course, you want to stay in the good graces of the powers that be, but do yourself a favor and don't create more work for yourself if you can avoid it.

So, what do you do when they ask and you're not grading it?

It's okay to be a little vague here. Say you might grade it. Say you haven't decided yet. The point is: you don't need to give students a straight answer every time.

Sometimes I just tell them after they finish, "I'm not grading this. #SorryNotSorry" And I leave it at that. Because you don't owe it to students to grade every single thing they do.

And who knows, not grading everything might actually help students develop a passion for learning for learning's sake.

At the end of the day, you'll still need to enter grades, and for that, we look to selective grading.

Selective Grading

If students know you only grade some things, they are more likely to do all things. It's like the intermittent rewards that you may have learned about in Psych 101. If we give a reward all the time, students will only be motivated when there is a reward. If we never give a reward, they aren't motivated at all.

The point is, normalize selective grading. Let students know you grade some assignments but not others. I have a friend who spins a wheel to determine which homework she will grade, and if you didn't do what the wheel lands on, you get a zero. Honestly, I think the wheel is genius, but I'm sure there are other ways to determine which one you'll grade. Maybe it's the one all the students did (get some points for our students that need them), maybe it's the one no one did, maybe you roll some dice to figure it out. No matter what you do, if you keep them guessing, you will likely get better results, and you won't have to grade everything, which is the goal!

This is very different though from not grading often, hardly grading, or effectively never grading. If you are just really late to put grades in, this is likely to create a scenario in which students don't value any of the work because you "never grade."

Speed Grading

One thing I love to do is use stamps. I go around and stamp the work immediately after doing it in class. This rewards the students who were doing what they were supposed to be doing and allows you to just check for the stamp later, when you're actually putting it in the gradebook. Yes, this is for completion assignments.

But anywhere I can save time and publicly let students know I'm checking is a win for me. I wish I had started using stamps earlier in my career. It's funny how now I use them with high school students and it brings them back to their elementary roots when they get that "great job" on their paper.

Speed Grading with Technology

As the saying goes, "work smarter, not harder." Why give yourself papers to grade when you can get technology to do it for you? Using tools such as Google Forms and other online quizzing applications allows you to grade multiple choice, true/false, and even short answers (sometimes and not always perfectly) in a flash. I LOVE using Google Forms when I can. It even has a screen lock feature now (it didn't always have that), which prevents students from opening other tabs while taking the quiz.

What if you want some writing? That's fine. Save yourself the time of grading all the right or wrong stuff by hand and only grade the short, long, or essay answers on the form.

They also keep data for you so you can see which questions are giving everyone a hard time. Sometimes I'll notice everyone missing a problem and then realize I forgot to teach it, so I throw it out or just give everyone the point for it. You can also see when that one student is missing all the questions that nearly everyone else is getting correct.

Using digital tools is a surefire way to speed up the grading and get the grades back to students sooner.

Grade One Problem, Not All of Them

Another clever secret is that you don't have to grade every problem the students do. You can even tell the class this when they turn it in, just announce, "I'm only looking at number 9," and let them know that is what you do sometimes. This works to save you time and incentivize students to do all of the problems, not knowing which one you're going to grade.

I do this all the time in social studies. I will give an assignment that has some definitions, some matching, let's say, and then there are one or two higher-order thinking questions at the end. I just graded those. (A) That's where the thinking happens, and (B) they wouldn't be able to answer those questions without doing the rest of the assignment.

Just grading one problem (or two, or three) will significantly cut down your grading time while allowing you to gather the data you need, whether or not your students actually learned anything.

Another version of this that I've used before is telling students, "I'm going to grade three of these, randomly." You don't have to say which ones. Just let them know that any of the questions could be selected, and that's what their score will be based on. Now students will have to do them all, but know up front that you're not going to grade them all. This could be discouraging and nerve-racking for some students, but at the end of the day, you're doing this to get grades in the gradebook faster, which the majority of your students are going to appreciate.

And if you want to level it up even more, let them pick which question they think they did best on. Have them circle it or put a star on it, and that's the one you grade. That lets students put their best foot forward and still gives you a quick check for understanding. The added bonus is that it builds some student agency into the process.

Grading doesn't have to be all or nothing. You're just trying a slice; you don't have to eat the whole cake.

How to Choose the Right Problem

You can do it randomly, but it will be a lot more meaningful and useful if you know what you're looking for. Find the problem, question, or whatever that really sums up the learning for the day. If it's math, it might be the one that really highlights the concept for the day; if it's ELA, it might be a thought-provoking short response or journal prompt.

I recently did this where I graded the first, middle, and last journal prompts for a book we were reading in economics. There was one for each chapter but journals being what they are, I didn't need to read all 14 to get a real picture of whether or not students were taking the time to think about the prompts or not.

No Homework for A's

Something that a teacher at my high school did, and this was back in the 1990s, was make it so you didn't have to do the homework if you got an A on the last test. As long as you were pulling A's on the assessments, you didn't have to do the daily assignments. That isn't to say that students didn't do the homework; some of them surely did to maintain their A's, but it means they didn't turn it in, which means he didn't have to grade it. This is what we call a classic win-win.

Batch Grading

When my wife was still teaching, she used to have all her students keep a binder. She taught high school biology, ninth grade, so not the most organized students in the world. However, she got them to keep a binder in the class, which was the only way for students to get grades outside of tests. She would then collect and grade the binders at set intervals. This would take her the whole night to grade, but she could just sit down with boxes of binders, knock it out in one night, and then be done grading for the next two weeks. That's what worked for her.

Something that has been working for me: one tactic I've deployed is collecting everything in file folders. I bought these cardboard hanging file folder holders and gave each student a file. This way, at the end of the nine weeks, or four and half weeks, or semester, whatever I feel like, I can just pull the student's file, check that they have the assigned classwork there, and then assign one grade. This is practical and useful for two reasons: one, it makes sure students don't lose their work—I just have them turn it into their folders at the end of class, and two, it allows me to put off grading every single thing they turn in.

If you're going to use the file folder system, though, you need to have a plan. When I first started this, I didn't have a system; I had a box full of files. Now my students are alphabetical and know which name is before and after them in class, so they can always find and put away their folder in the same spot. This might be a procedure you'll have to teach, but this is one of those "anything worth doing is worth doing right" situations, and I can't stress enough how much better my life is now that students have stopped "losing" their folders.

Remember, though, this is supposed to save you time, not make your job harder. You need to have a system that works for you.

Speaking of batch grading, there is an added bonus as well. By grading all the assignments at once, or at least a chunk of them, you're better able to see patterns in students' work. You can see who is getting it and who isn't, just be sure you don't wait so long that you lose students who need that extra help. When you're grading this way, the patterns just naturally emerge; you're looking at paper after paper that says the same thing, and then suddenly you notice something that doesn't fit. You're then able to address that later in class and give those students the support they need the most.

Combining this with selective grading, feel free to only grade some of the papers in the batch as well. Maybe you collect 12 worksheets that you have done in class throughout the past three weeks but you're only looking at the three high-leverage ones. This is a way of combining these concepts to work for you and protect your mental health and time.

Feedback Is Food for Growth

My opinion, and it might not be a popular one, is that if students are writing something lengthy, then you owe them some feedback. If they take the time to write you a three-page essay, then you can write a paragraph telling them how they did and where they can improve. It doesn't have to be long, but it needs to be something. In this age of AI and other writing helpers, students are becoming increasingly poor writers. A little feedback can go a long way in helping them to improve in this vital, and diminishing, skill.

That being said, if the students answered ten multiple-choice questions and you marked four of them incorrect, that's feedback too, and in my opinion, again, enough feedback. You don't need to write to the student that they answered "C" when in fact the correct answer was "D." The student, seeing the red line, X, or however you grade it, is good enough; they'll get the point.

Compliment Sandwich

Maybe you've heard of this, maybe you haven't, but sometimes I find students are not great at constructive criticism. In this day and age of grade inflation and helicopter parents, they don't always take to the idea that they can do better. So, what do I do? I use the compliment sandwich when giving the goods to a student.

A compliment sandwich, as the name implies, is when you sandwich the negative feedback in between two pieces of compliments. It might look something like this:

> Your thesis was really strong and a great way to open your essay. Your third paragraph didn't really relate back to your thesis and was a little muddled. Great conclusion relating it back to your topic sentence and tying it all together.

That's it. Think of it as "good, bad, good" if you will. Even if a paper, product, or assignment is really bad, and there's not a lot to praise, I still only give the student one thing to work on. Most aren't going to listen to a laundry list of faults, so stick to one thing they can improve on each time and move on.

Verbal Feedback

An easy way to give feedback is to give verbal feedback to students. This is usually done after they answer a question in class. Try to give specific feedback on what they have shared with the class. Too often, teachers (I'm guilty of this too from time to time) just say "nice answer" or "good job" but don't really give the student feedback on what was said. Try to demonstrate active listening and give the student some specific feedback, such as "Great job including X in your answer" or "that was a solid response. You summarized all the points of Y very well." It's easy and doesn't feel that different, but it does give that little something extra to the feedback to (A) let the student know what was proficient in their response and (B) model for the rest of the class what a solid answer looks like.

Non-Verbal Feedback

I'm a big fan of giving a fist bump or high five for solid answers and attempts in the classroom. Sure, they don't give any usable data to the student for further improvement, but they sure do make people feel good. And in the classroom, where relationships are key, there's nothing wrong with spreading around some dopamine to students for a job well done.

Voice Memos

Depending on which Learning Management System (LMS) you are using for students to turn in work, voice memos are a great way to save time. Tools like Mote allow you to record your feedback and post it on a Google Doc as a voice memo. This is great if you aren't great at typing or need to save time, and it also allows students to hear your voice and hopefully take feedback a little better based on your tone.

Sticky Feedback

When it comes to giving private feedback in class, I love using sticky notes. They let me say what needs to be said without making a scene. I've written notes like "Do you need to go to the nurse?" when I notice a student with their head down or acting off, and "Do I need to call home?" when a student keeps acting up, but I want to avoid a power struggle. Writing a quick note and dropping it off as I walk through the room is one of my favorite low-drama ways to redirect behavior.

You can also use sticky notes to give quiet praise, especially for shy students who hate being called out in front of their classmates.

Other ideas for sticky notes:

Redirects/Behavior Nudges

- "Why don't you step out for a sec and come back when you're ready?"
- "This behavior is headed towards a phone call home."

Check-ins/Support

- "You, okay? You've been really quiet today."
- "I'm not trying to pry, but if you need anything, let me know."

Positive Reinforcement

- "You've been locked in today. Just wanted you to know I see it."
- "You've been way more focused lately, keep that streak going."

Give Yourself a Deadline

An easy way to motivate yourself to grade is to give yourself a deadline. If you're like me, and if you're still reading, I'm sure you might be, you grade better when the grades must be turned in, like the end of a term or grading window.

The easiest way to give yourself a deadline is to make a commitment to your students. Tell them when they turn in some paper or take a test, I will have these graded by next week, or tomorrow, or whatever you come up with, but make it known. (Additionally, there is research about making "prior commitments" that we're more likely to stick to things if you commit to a timeline, you're more likely to stick to it.) No one wants to let down 100 students by not having their grades done when you said they would be, and the real grade grubbers in the room will be on your ass if you don't get it done when you say you will. What could be more motivating? Anyway, that's it. Announce to your students when you will have it graded, and you're more likely to grade it.

Realistic Timelines

Know thyself, as the saying goes. Don't commit to grading all their term papers over your weekend or getting things back to them in a day if you can't pull it off. Set the deadline but give yourself enough breathing room to pull it off, too. If that means you tell them "These essays will be graded in two weeks," then you tell them two weeks, the point is that you created the deadline, and you're going to try to stick to it.

When You Are Just Overwhelmed

I once let essays, which were just a formative essay, sit on my desk for two months. You know what I did at the end of the two months? I threw them away. Sure, that sucks for the students but the truth is I waited too long to grade them for the students to get any meaningful insights from my feedback. If this happens to you, or you're just overwhelmed and sitting there with five worksheets to grade, four homework, and a test, throw something out. It doesn't help anyone to get an 8/10 on a worksheet that they finished a month ago. Just don't grade it. The purpose of grades, outside of school mandates, should be to improve, and no one is improving with month-old feedback.

> The purpose of grades, outside of school mandates, should be to improve.

Averaging, Curving, and Grade Inflation

Whether you're an "easy" grader or a "hard" grader, at some point, you're going to encounter the question of whether or not you should curve an assignment.

I always curve a test when no one gets a perfect score. That is rare. I usually always have some perfect scores, which I give out little trophies for, so my curve is usually set at the default, but when it's not, I curve. Why do I curve? If someone is not getting a perfect score, then that tells me I wasn't the perfect teacher; I created the opportunity for an information gap. Maybe my pacing was off, maybe I had a sub one day, I don't know, but somehow information was missed.

Whereas a perfect score reinforces what I have done in the classroom, it tells me, "At some point I covered everything," but on an exam where the highest is like a 90%, I'm thinking I must not have missed the mark at some point. In that case, I curve.

What to Do When Everyone Bombs

Sometimes we give an assignment or assessment, and everyone bombs it. That might (will?) happen at some point to you. The best thing you can do here is throw it out and reteach and retest. There's no shame in it, and your students will thank you for it. If, for some reason, you can't throw it out, you can curve it as well.

However, if all your students are failing, there is something going on in the classroom that needs to be addressed. This could be an instructional gap, such as you didn't cover the material, or it might relate to classroom management or some other issue going on.

My first year teaching, I was just coming in over the heads of my eighth graders having come from student-teaching high school, and they were all struggling with my lesson.

How to Curve

In case no one has ever told you how to curve an assignment, I'm going to share what I do.

There are many methods to curve, but the one that works for me is to take the highest grade in the class, say it's a 95%, and make that the 100%. Now, everyone else gets a plus 5% to their grade. That's it, pretty simple.

There are other methods where you can use the mean to curve, but I think rewarding the student who did the best helps, and what I like about this is it doesn't move the goal post that much, usually.

Dropping the Lowest
Another way to curve a student's grade is to drop their lowest grade. It could be a zero from something they didn't do, or just something they biffed. Either way, dropping their lowest score

will "inflate" their grade a bit, but sometimes we gotta do that. I'm not going to lie to you, grades matter a lot to students, their families, but especially to administrators and counselors. I once had a counselor say that she loved grade inflation because it made her job easier. This is what you're up against, and you're not going to win this fight alone. I'm not saying to lean into grade inflation, I'm saying if you're bumping a few points by dropping a zero, you're probably doing yourself a favor more than the student.

Test Corrections and Retakes

When it comes to grading, I hate test corrections. They are annoying to grade and figure out. I have given .5 for corrections and as high as .8 for corrections, when it comes to getting points back on a question. However, when it comes to learning, test corrections are important. We should want students to go back over and correct their mistakes. We should want students to strive for excellence. So, even though it's a pain, it's a pain I recommend you take on.

Group and Partner Grading

How do we assign a grade when more than one student is working on it? Well, there are a couple of ways to do it, but I'll share what works for me.

The first thing I do is define what a group grade is and what an individual grade is. Maybe the presentation is a group grade, but each individual has to turn in their own research. Or maybe you assign different parts of the presentation to different members and grade them based on that. That's the first step.

The next thing I do is, whenever possible, I have students turn things in using a Google product. What is nice about Google Docs and Google Slides is that you can see what everyone contributes. If I click on a slide deck and the only thing you did was type your name, you're not getting the same grade as everyone else in the group. I'll admit, using Google is more likely to take points away than award points, but it is a way to hold students accountable, which is what we want when doing group projects. We've all seen the memes about group work, and no one wants one person getting credit for something they didn't do.

The third thing I do to help with accountability is I give a survey at the end of each project, where group members get to privately grade each member of their group. They say what grade they deserve and why. It's an easy way to find out who was pulling their weight and who was dragging everyone down.

So that's it. Clearly state what grade you're assigning to whom, use a system of accountability, and then have students grade their teammates.

Then just take all that and apply it to partners as well.

An added tip, for in-class partner work, is to sometimes have partners use different color pens or markers. This also allows you to see who did what.

Rubrics

There's a myth around rubrics that has always bugged me. The myth is that having a rubric makes your assignment automatically objective. Sometimes that's true, but other times it is not.

Here's an example: say the rubric language says "cites all sources in MLA format," that is objective. Perfect. But say it says something like "Maintains eye contact with the audience" or "speaks clearly," well, those are more subjective. And sometimes, because we know the students, they become even more subjective where we end up thinking "that was good eye contact... for her" or "that was speaking clearly... for him" and then at that point we might as well just throw the papers on the stairs and give all the ones that end up at the top an A.

So, what should you do? Should we still use rubrics? Yes, yes, you should. Just accept that there is some ambiguity built into it. Just because it's a rubric doesn't absolve you of having to make judgment calls; it just sets the lines for where those judgments fall.

Rubrics are fantastic for two main reasons. The first is that it forces you to quantify the end product. This is what we talked about in the lesson planning chapter. By creating your rubric when you create the assignment, you are forcing yourself to think about what mastery looks like. You're creating a clear image of how you will know if your students learned or not.

The second reason is that a rubric allows students to know what criteria they will be evaluated against, and this is crucial for students who want to get the highest marks. They can see, in black and white, where they will land given their assignment. Yes, there might be some subjective wording, but it will at the very least give them guidance on which direction to go.

How to Use Rubrics

Rubrics make grading and feedback faster. One way I use rubrics for feedback is just to highlight the language on the rubric where the student's assignment falls. This tells them how they did when I passed it back without me having to write up a bunch of feedback.

A second way to use rubrics is to have students grade themselves first. This allows for some valuable self-reflection. If a student scores themselves lower on the rubric, you can be sure they know it isn't 100% material. Oftentimes, students will be harsher on themselves than we are, which can boost their self-esteem when they get their grades back. You do run the risk of scoring them lower than they scored themselves, as well, but with the appropriate amount of feedback, this should be a great learning experience for them.

Final Thoughts

Grading is a beast. We've covered that. But you don't have to let it run your life. If you take anything from this chapter, let it be to grade less, grade what matters, and give meaningful feedback.

There are many strategies covered in this chapter and hopefully you'll find something that works for you. You don't need to try them all at once but give them a go and if one isn't working for you, stop doing that and try another. I'm confident you'll find your stride.

When it comes to feedback, keep it simple. Give students one thing to work on or try next time. Too much feedback and the message will get lost.

At the end of the day, while grades are required, it is growth we're looking for in our students. If you can make grading less of a grind and give solid feedback, you're on your way to making grading suck less.

Chapter Recap
- Don't grade everything, focus on mastery.
- Use selective grading or tools to speed up grading.
- Feedback doesn't have to be long to be effective.
- Use rubrics to help students know what to focus on, and make grading easier.
- Don't take grading home (unless completely necessary).

5

Suck Less at Burnout: How to Stay Up When You're Under Water

Teacher burnout is at an all-time high. You don't have to look far on the internet or social media to see that teachers are stressed out and overworked. Everywhere I look there are teachers feeling unsupported and leaving the profession. Heck, you might be one of them and maybe you picked up this book as a last-ditch effort to find something to hang onto. If that is the case, I hope I've been able to help.

There are teacher shortages across the nation, and things are not looking any better. These shortages are leading to larger class sizes, which increase daily stress loads. They lead to teachers taking on more responsibilities, which leads to more exhaustion. They lead to teachers taking on more of the emotional load of helping students when they have fewer people to turn to, which leads to feeling stressed or drained. Everywhere you look, it's like the chips are stacked against us.

Regardless of what kind of school you're at, you're going to need to battle burnout in all its many forms and attacks. Burnout creeps up like a fungus. You don't notice it at first. Then one day you're standing in front of your classroom, completely out of it, counting the days until the weekend, and it's only Tuesday.

Burnout hits all teachers at some point. Whether you're in year one or year twenty-one, it's coming for you, so you're going to need to figure out how to manage it.

A lot of what is in this chapter could feel condescending at first glance if you're feeling like a failure every day to your students. The practices and suggestions in this chapter are not a cure for real mental anguish or health issues. I would suggest seeking the help of a licensed mental health professional for serious issues. The guidance below is to help address burnout in education and hopefully help you make it through the school year a little less on the end of your rope.

> **Professional Help**
>
> Speaking of professional help, if you're at a school with decent health insurance, you should have access to mental health services. Some schools even have specified services in addition to insurance. Take advantage of your resources. There is no shame in needing someone to hear you vent and help you through the stress of the job, and whatever else you have going on.

1,500 Decisions

Teachers make an astonishing number of daily choices. *Education Week* once estimated that teachers make as many as 1,500 decisions per day (Klein, 2021). Multiply that by five times a week, and you can see why we want to just veg out when we get home from school. Of course, we go home, plop on the sofa, and stream endlessly through the Netflix menu; we're spent. We have to decide which battles are worth fighting each day; do you need to respond to that email before or after lunch, when is the best time to let Johnny sharpen his pencil without interrupting the lesson, how much time will you have for lunch if you have to make copies, etc., etc., etc. These micro-decisions drain your mental battery, what psychologists call "decision fatigue." Every choice chips away at your willpower, and by the end of the day, you're running on fumes.

And those 1,500 decisions? That's *just* the classroom stuff. That doesn't include deciding what to wear, what to prep the night before, which route you're taking to school, and whether or not you should stop off for a latte in the morning. When you take into account all the decisions you have to make just to function in a day, it really adds up.

There is something to be done, though. Take as many decisions out of the day as you can. Maybe you have a set time when students can go to the bathroom, and they can just grab the pass and go without having to ask. Or you could set up clear procedures around sharpening pencils, throwing away paper, or getting a tissue. Think about what procedures you can put in place to eliminate decisions you have to make. The more you can front-load the mental task of making decisions, the less burned out you'll be in the long run.

> The more you can front-load the mental task of making decisions, the less burned out you'll be in the long run.

Signs You're Burning Out

There are many signs of teacher burnout, and it hits everyone a little differently. See how you're holding up below:

- You've been more cynical than usual (you've upped your snark quota and you're not sure why).
- Minor inconveniences send you into a spiral (tech issues, losing your planning period, a kid getting up without asking).
- You've picked up some unhealthy coping habits (eating too much, drinking too much, sleeping too much … or barely sleeping at all).
- You've withdrawn from your coworkers or your students (lights off, door shut, lunch alone, don't-talk-to-me withdrawn).

- You're constantly irritable and on edge (you're snapping at students for little things or worse, blowing up on your boss).
- You've started feeling depressed or hopeless.
- You've stopped doing core parts of the job (lesson planning, grading, even taking attendance).

If any of this sounds familiar, know that you're not alone. Burnout is incredibly common for teachers (and others in jobs like ours, think doctors). This list is by no means exhaustive, and you may experience burnout differently; these are just a few of the ways that I have experienced it in the past.

Physical Burnout

I know we just talked about signs of burnout, but I thought we should take a moment to consider burnout and what it does to our bodies. Teaching is physically demanding. You're on your feet most of the day, holding your pee for six hours, and probably eating your lunch like a recruit at boot camp. It's hard.

You've got to take care of yourself first, or you're useless to anyone else. At the risk of sounding cliché, you gotta put your mask on first.

Some signs you might be physically burned out:

- Your back is tight, sore, or otherwise saying "no."
- You're in a constant state of recovery, but never fully well.
- You're getting headaches all the time.
- You're getting the gut bubbles that mean something is not right.

No one needs a teacher martyr, and they don't give out medals for powering through with the flu or a tweaked back. Take time to rest, it's not a weakness but being fair to yourself as a person first and a teacher second.

So, what can you do when your body starts waving the white flag?

- Go for a walk during your planning period.
- Make sure you're actually eating lunch *and* giving yourself time to chew.
- Take a sick day when you're sick. Pushing through it helps no one. (The students will be okay.)
- Stretch.
- Get more sleep, when you can. Don't sacrifice sleep to grade papers or lesson plan. That stuff will come.

The work will be there when you return (which might fill you with more dread), but at least you'll be better able to address it. Take a break. Get some rest. Teaching is a marathon and not a sprint.

Emotional Boundaries

It's weird how nowhere in the job description of being a teacher does it say that we have to be there for our students empathetically, emotionally, or in any capacity outside of our role as the teacher, but we all know it is there in some form or another.

Every teacher sets up their emotional boundaries differently. Some tell their students everything, eat lunch with students, and listen to all their drama. Others have built a wall around themselves and taken steps to shield themselves from the chaos that is working with growing children. Whichever approach you take, the job will take a toll on you emotionally, and you're going to need to know how to set healthy boundaries. Boundaries aren't about walls; they're about taking care of yourself.

Setting up emotional boundaries is going to be key to reducing burnout. Finding out just what you can handle is the best way to make sure you don't give too much of yourself. As I have mentioned before, I use my clothing as one way to establish this. I have a clear "Mr. Glassford" outfit that I wear to work, and when I get home and change into my "civilian" clothes, I shed a lot of what is bothering me for the day. It's not perfect, and some things you can't let go of, but it helps.

Keep Your Lunch for You

One rule I set up really early on in my career was the idea that lunch was my time. I do not allow students or the school to take a second of my 30 minutes. Sure, over the course of my nearly 20 years, I have made exceptions, but 99% of the time, that half hour is dedicated to me. Find a way not to work during your lunch if you can. Don't hold students to talk to after class, and take lunchtime for yourself. Don't schedule meetings during your lunch, and don't go to meetings during your lunch. It's likely that in your state, you are allowed a lunch. If you have a union, you almost certainly have a protected lunchtime. Take it. Keep it for you. This little respite will help stave off burnout and hopefully allow you to take a much-needed break.

Saying "Yes" to Yourself

As Steven Covey explains in *The 7 Habits of Highly Effective People*, to say "yes" to something is to say "no" to something else (Covey, 1989, pp. 156–158). The reverse is also true, when you say "no" you're saying "yes" to things that really matter to you. When you say no to covering a class during your planning period, you're saying yes to getting your papers graded or your copies made (or just getting to use the bathroom without feeling rushed). When you say no to sponsoring a new club, staying late for a meeting, or anything else that is being asked of you, what you're really doing is saying yes to your mental health.

You need to get comfortable with saying no to things. One way to do this is to stop viewing it as being negative or not a "team player" and instead remember what you're saying yes to. Even if all you're saying yes to is vegging out on the couch, rewatching *The Office* for the fourth time, it doesn't matter. That is still your time.

You will always be asked to do more, and if you're not careful, before you know it, you'll be doing it all. You'll be on all the committees, sponsor all the clubs, coach all the teams... not really, but you can see where this is going. Ever heard the expression "If you want something done, give it to a busy person?" The trick is to strike the right balance and say yes to the things that spark joy for you. If you truly want to do something, do it. If the money you get for subbing during your plan is worth it to you and you view it more as a case of beer and less as a case of suck, by all means, cover the class.

But I'm telling you, you have my permission to say no. Saying no to the extras helps you say yes to showing up with energy for your actual students. They don't need you to be burnt out, they need you to be present.

You don't have to give a TED Talk when you say no. Try these:

- "If I weren't already at capacity, I would love to help."
- "I'm sorry, but that isn't something I can take on now."
- "I need to protect my planning period today, but thank you for asking."

You're not being rude. You're being clear.

I've had plenty of teachers tell me no when asking them to help out with a project I am working on, a club I'm running, or an event I'm putting on. At the end of the day, this is a hate-the-game, not the player situation. Teaching is hard work, and I respect that they are able to tell me no. Besides, I'd rather have a no than someone who is going to half-ass a commitment.

At one school I was at, there was a teacher who did it all because she thought no one else would. She sponsored the Lunar New Year Event, organized our Black History Month Event, led the students on field trips, headed up Spirit Week, went to every meeting she was asked to attend, and even joined the school leadership team. You want to guess what happened to her and what she is doing now? She's burned out. Now she just does her job. She got stretched so thin she snapped. You can't be the only one marching in the band.

On the flip side, I knew a teacher who only ran the student government. She said no all the freaking time. She even had a shirt (and I swear on my mother I'm not making this up) that just said "No!" on it. She would wear it about once a week.

> The trick is not in saying "no" to everything, but in saying "yes" to the things that fill you up.

But she did say yes to one thing, and she loved that thing. She poured herself into student government, and it paid dividends to her mental health. Sure, she had to run homecoming, the talent show, and host meetings and fundraisers, but she didn't see it as work because it was her yes. The trick is not in saying "no" to everything, but in saying "yes" to the things that fill you up, not the things that drill a hole in your bucket.

You have to learn to say no and let others pick up the slack sometimes.

Sponsor Your Club

One great way to combat burnout is to sponsor a club. I know it sounds counterintuitive to do more work to feel less burned out, but it's true. Getting to see students in a different light can do wonders for the soul and rekindle the light in you that might be going out. Seeing students interact with something they're passionate about and that brings them joy will remind you of why you got into this in the first place.

I've worked at many schools, and they all have different approaches to clubs. You may or may not get paid but regardless of what kind of school you're at, my advice remains the same. Sponsor a club. Sorry, scratch that, sponsor your club. Find or create a club that brings you joy that you can share with students.

I've seen podcasting clubs, Anime clubs, pottery clubs, origami clubs, you name it, and I've seen them take off. In my time as a teacher, I've been a class sponsor, a student government sponsor, a Natural Helpers leader, a morning announcement club (we didn't think of a clever name for this one), and even a Dungeons and Dragons club.

Hell, I even sponsored the chess club for two weeks before I realized it was not the club for me and passed it off to a different teacher. But that's my point, chess wasn't my jam, so I ditched it. You need to create a club that is something you enjoy. Even if it's making Disney princesses out of macaroni, create your club.

It'll be that breath of fresh air when the classroom has you down. It'll be your sanctuary when you feel like none of your students like you. It'll be a chance for you to be you, while still being a teacher.

Protect Your Time and Your Weekends, Too

One thing I make sure I don't do is reply to emails after 5 pm. I give a small buffer to things that come in right after school, but if it's after 5 pm, it has to wait until the next day. And guess what? The world keeps spinning.

When you make yourself available at all hours, people start expecting you to be available at all hours. It's a fast track to burnout. Researchers from Virginia Tech found that just the expectation of after-hours email, not even checking it, spikes anxiety and disrupts work-life balance (Belkin, Becker, & Conroy, 2016). So even seeing that little notification pops up while you're trying to enjoy dinner can derail your whole evening.

You have to be able to unplug from work. In fact, unplugging is so essential that the freaking French passed a law about it, employees there have the "right to disconnect" and ignore after-hours emails without consequences. Wild, right?

Your home time is for you. Not your principal. Not coworkers. Not parents. And certainly not students.

I get emails from students after 5 pm (sometimes even at 10 pm) all the time. That's when it is convenient for them to send the email. I reply when it is convenient for me.

And as my buddy used to say, "Poor planning on your part does not make an emergency on mine."

This goes double, no, triple (maybe even quadruple), for weekends. While we do get plenty of time off during the year as teachers, the weekends are still our time. You are under no obligation to email someone back on Saturday or Sunday. The weekends are your time to recharge so you can show up for the very people trying to get hold of you.

This behavior, of not replying to emails, is not being a poor employee. No one is going to call you into the office and ask why you didn't respond at 8 pm on Wednesday to the email. Email is for non-urgent matters. If they need a response right then and there, they can pick up the phone and call you.

The key here is to set up that boundary right away. Simply by not replying, which again you don't have to do, you're saying without saying, "My time is my time."

Turn Off Notifications

Set your phone to silent when you get home. If you can't do that, turn off notifications. There is no email, Slack, or other communication that you are reasonably required to reply to during off-hours. What will likely happen is that a student, a parent, or a principal will email you with a question after hours, or someone will make a snarky Slack comment, or the like. And it'll become like an earworm you can't stop thinking about, so you'll want to respond. I've already mentioned that you don't want to get in the habit of being known to be someone who replies after hours. But what's going to happen when you get that notification is it'll flip your brain into work mode and start siphoning off mental energy.

You have a computer at work for email and notifications. Keep your email off your phone if you can. Keep it all off your device if you can. That way you can check it when you're at work, in work mode, and if need be, can ask someone for clarity or advice before responding.

This isn't just about logging off or self-preservation; this is about mental health as well. According to researchers at UC Irvine, "people in the interrupted conditions experienced a higher workload, more stress, higher frustration, more time pressure, and effort" (Mark, Gudith, & Klocke, 2008). Not to mention the added stress it brings.

Even if we don't respond, we start composing the reply in our heads, over dinner, in the shower, while trying to sleep. I don't know about you, but I fixate on the emails I get. If I look at my email after I get home, I'll want to respond to every one of them. If a parent emails me on a Saturday, I'll spend all weekend thinking about it.

That's why I've taken my own advice and removed my email from my phone. I don't need it pinging me every time someone has an issue. My time is mine, and I recommend the same for you.

Stop Taking Work Home (You're Not Going to Do)

There's nothing more shame-inducing than a sack full of papers that need to be graded sitting by your door. Give yourself the break you need to disconnect from school. A little honesty about what you're actually willing to do at home will go a long way for your mental health.

When I first started teaching, I used to haul home a literal box of ungraded papers, full of good intentions. But by the time I ate (always starving after school), walked the dog, and caught my breath, it was after 7 pm, and grading just wasn't going to happen. Then, in the morning, I would lug the papers back to school. This routine repeated itself until I finally ran up against a deadline that forced my hand. Eventually, I realized: if I didn't grade it at school, I wasn't going to grade it at home.

Maybe you're someone who loves taking work home and spending every time on work stuff outside of school. But if you're reading this chapter, chances are you're feeling burnout creeping in, which tells me it's time to stop. The work will still be there in the morning. That's what planning periods are for.

Maximize Your Planning Period

One way to prevent burnout, and it feels a bit like an uphill battle when you're struggling to keep your head above water, is to maximize your planning period and not use it for turning your brain off. We're going to accomplish this with a few simple moves.

First, close your door. The open door invites people in. It could be students, another teacher, or whoever. Having an open door says, "hey, come bother me," and that is the last thing we want. Close your door during your plan, and you'll see an increase in productivity.

Second, put your phone away. Go ahead and give yourself a few minutes to check your missed texts or calls, and then put your phone in your bag, a desk drawer, or just turn it off. The phone, especially social media, can suck our time away and limit our productivity. Put the phone down and get to work.

Third, create a list of everything you want to get done during your planning period. (I like to put "make a list" at the top of my lists so I can start by checking something off and get a little dopamine boost. Nothing feels better than starting ahead of the game.) Write down all the things you need to get done on that list. It might make it feel like you'll never get it all done, and you might not, but it will serve as a guide and reminder to keep you on task.

I'm not saying never take a break on your prep. Sometimes you need to refill that cup of joe or go for a walk, but if you spend it hanging around the teachers' lounge every single planning period, then you're never going to get to what you need to get done and thus are more likely to feel overwhelmed and burnt out.

During my first years as a teacher, I was guilty about not using my planning periods effectively. I would hang out with my teacher friends, leave school for a coffee, take a nap (yes, I did this a few times), or just play on my phone. I would do all these things to escape my work, but end up leaving me with just as much work to do, but having half as much time to do it in. Now I have to take work home, or just have a daunting, ever-expanding pile of work to get to each day when I come to work. It wasn't until later that I learned that using my plan for work and getting stuff done was the best way to help me relax and feel refreshed at the end of my day. And not dread coming into work each morning as much either.

Phoning It In

When all else fails, though, sometimes you just need a quiet Monday. These are the days when you pop on a movie, pass out a packet, do some silent reading, and just sit at your desk and meditate. Not literally, but turn it off while still getting paid. It's okay. You're there, your students are accounted for, and some learning is still technically taking place.

These days can be tricky depending on how vigilant your administration is, but I'm here to reassure you and tell you that we've all been there. Sometimes, popping on a 45-minute video is the only way to maintain your sanity, and it's still more effective than having a sub. Don't feel bad if you have to phone it in now and again; there's no shame in that game.

Now, I would be remiss if I didn't add the caveat that these days should be fewer and further between than the norm, and if they are becoming that way, then what you might need is a full recharge. See below.

PTO

If movie day isn't working for you, sometimes you just need to stay home or stay in bed to stay sane.

Last I checked, no one is handing out trophies for "teacher with the most unused personal days." If you have found yourself feeling overwhelmed by the day-to-day and phoning it in isn't working, and none of the other above strategies have seemed to help, then give yourself a break. Take the day off. The kids will be okay. Sometimes we call these your "mental health days." Hell, at one school I worked at, you actually got two mental health days a year (on top of your personal days a year). The point is, teachers need a break, and the students take days off, so why shouldn't we?

So, stay up late on a Sunday and take Monday off, or take a Wednesday, or a three-day weekend. Do what you need to do to show up recharged and ready to go. My two cents, schools wouldn't give you days that don't roll over if they didn't want you to use them.

This goes double for sick days. While some districts may roll those over each year, very few pay them out at the end of your career. You might want them to do the old "call off until the end of the year" play that I've seen some older teachers do, but if you're sick, you're sick, and you shouldn't be at school. Especially, post-COVID. Take the day off and get some rest.

Self-Care

Is there a term more overused these days than "self-care?" I sort of secretly hate the term because it feels like it can be used to blame you for situations that someone else created, in the way our society asks so much from our teachers. It's like, sure, the toxic emails at 9 pm are a problem, but instead of fixing the system, admin tells us to go meditate and "do self-care." That's not care. That's gaslighting, and it needs to stop. Not everything can be fixed with a pizza party, and sometimes you have to, unfortunately, take matters into your own hands.

Everything we've been talking about in this chapter is a form of self-care. Saying "no," sponsoring the club you want to sponsor, and not replying to emails after school or on weekends. Those are all self-care.

I can't stress this enough, though, you need to find time for yourself, especially in those first few years teaching. I started tanning my first year (don't worry, I don't anymore), but I was able to crawl into the machine and just turn my mind off while I was irradiated for 20 minutes. Sure, I ended up looking like a contestant on Love Island, but it was relaxing.

Join a gym, do yoga, take up running; you have to find something to stay active and get your mind out of the classroom. But there is self-care at work, too. Maybe dipping out during your prep for a latte is self-care, or bringing your own lunch to school, or maybe self-care is Door Dashing, your favorite Chinese spot for lunch. You have to decide what brings you joy, and only you can decide what that is. I'm just telling you to find that joy. You'll need it. That little respite from the poop storm that is teaching in the 21st century.

Dr. Pooja Lakshmin argues in *Real Self-Care* that many of the practices we call "self-care" are really "faux self-care" meaning they aren't a real solution to your problems (Lakshmin, 2023).

She argues that the little breaks we give ourselves aren't going to solve our daily burnout, and she is probably right. But like most things in education, you gotta fake it till you make it ... to the end of the day. There is a systemic issue in education where teachers are constantly asked to do more with less. For our own peace of mind, though, we'll need to focus on what is in our control. Think of these things like "burnout band-aids" and not "the solution to all work problems."

While you probably don't need me to say any of this, I think you should take a second, though, and make a mental note of when you selfishly took time for yourself last. If it is becoming fewer and farther between, you're heading for a crash.

You're not weak for needing to treat yourself. Even the toughest teachers need a break now and again. It's not about giving everything, but about saving yourself so you still have something to give.

Done for Now

When burnout strikes, you sometimes just have to be done for now. There is an expression you've likely heard that "done is better than perfect," and that is what teaching is nowadays. You have to get comfortable being "done for now" and moving on. Is the lesson perfect? Likely not. Are all the papers graded with feedback? Doesn't matter. What matters is that you're able to sustainably exist in this field you've chosen without breaking down and quitting. The world needs good teachers, and if you're taking the time to read a book on teaching, you're already one of the good ones.

If I've said it once, I've said it a million times: "Being a good teacher is deciding what you're not going to get done." I used to say this when I was a coach and would literally tell teachers to let some things go. Being a teacher is deciding what not to do. Lessons will always be able to be tweaked. Your slide deck can always be fixed.

> What matters is that you're able to sustainably exist in this field you've chosen without breaking down and quitting.

Parents will always need to be called. Your desk will always need to be cleaned. Copies to be made, a room to be reorganized, or a textbook to be read. There is always more to do. The system is broken in ways our bosses quietly acknowledge, and they know the task is impossible. That's why getting it "done for now" is sometimes the best and only move. Figure out what you're okay with not doing, what you can live with leaving until later or not at all, and let it go. Letting go isn't giving up, it's survival. It's choosing yourself over self-sacrifice.

If you don't believe me, think about how many "bad" teachers exist in the world. Seriously. All the teachers who forget to take attendance, show a movie every other day, just lecture their students for 90 minutes, the ones that really are just going through the motions... You got one? They still have a job, don't they? You can let a few things slip through the cracks and still keep your job. And better yet, thrive. Trust me on this.

Burnout Prevention Plan

If you're still with me, I hope you found something that helps (whether that's getting through the day, the week, the year, or just limping to the next three-day weekend), whatever works. The point is, I hope you found something useful. As stated previously, burnout comes in many shapes, sizes, and forms, and affects us all a little differently. But hopefully, with a little work, we can prevent burnout for as long as possible. I call this my burnout prevention plan.

- ♦ Boundary Setting
  - What are your non-negotiables? (Think email after 5 pm or no students during lunch.)
  - What are you *not* willing to take home? (Like grading or thinking about that kid in your fifth period who just will not stop talking.)
- ♦ Emotional Maintenance
  - Who is your best "teacher buddy" that you can vent to? (Maybe it's not a teacher, or not a teacher at your

school, but someone who will let you get it all out into the open.)
- How will you check in with your own mental health weekly? (What will you do to recognize "burnout creep?")
- Saying "no" and protecting your time
  - How will you maximize your time at work to minimize time out of work? (Think about using planning periods effectively, or the time before students arrive.)
  - What are you going to choose not to do? (Email parents, modify old slides, write three paragraphs of feedback on every paper.)
- Finding Joy
  - What will you do to find joy outside of the classroom? (Sponsor a club, attend a school game, find a new hobby.)
  - What small practice will you implement to bring you joy? (Weekly latte, taking a walk, doing a silly warm-up in class.)
- Physical Burnout
  - How will you maintain your body? (Stretch, eat a real lunch—slowly, get some sleep.)
  - What signs will you look for and how will you respond?
- Peak Burnout
  - When you've had enough, how will you react? When the above stops working, who will you call? What will you do?

You don't have to do it all to be a good teacher, but you do have to take care of yourself so you can show up for students. So, before you get burned out again, make a plan. Write it down. Put it on a Post-it note on the mirror in the bathroom. Or wherever you're likely to see it when you need it. Burnout may never disappear, but with a plan, you can face it head-on and suck a little less tomorrow.

Chapter Recap

- Burnout comes for us all. Be ready and be kind to yourself.
- Take some decisions off your plate when you can.
- Don't ignore the signs of burnout.
- Say "Yes" to yourself.
- Protect your time.
- Maintain balance (silence notifications, don't take work home).
- Take time off when you need it.
- Make a prevention plan.

References

Belkin, L. Y., Becker, W. J., & Conroy, S. A. (2016). Exhausted, but unable to disconnect: After-hours email, work-family balance and identification. *Academy of Management Proceedings, 2016*(1), Article 10353. https://journals.aom.org/doi/10.5465/AMBPP.2016.10353abstract

Covey, S. R. (1989). *The 7 habits of highly effective people: Powerful lessons in personal change*. Free Press.

Klein, A. (2021, December 6). 1,500 decisions a day (at least!): How teachers cope. *Education Week*. https://www.edweek.org/teaching-learning/1-500-decisions-a-day-at-least-how-teachers-cope-with-a-dizzying-array-of-questions/2021/12

Lakshmin, P. (2023). *Real self-care: A transformative program for redefining wellness*. Penguin Life.

Mark, G., Gudith, D., & Klocke, U. (2008). The cost of interrupted work: More speed and stress. In *Proceedings of the SIGCHI Conference on Human Factors in Computing Systems* (pp. 107–110). ACM. https://doi.org/10.1145/1357054.1357072

6

Suck Less Together: Building Community and Support Structures That Last

It might sound weird since you're surrounded by people all day, but if you really think about it, teaching can be pretty isolating. Like, how much time do we actually get to spend with our coworkers? Lunchtime, maybe a few minutes in the hallway? During in-service week or professional development days? But how much do we really get to talk to our coworkers or just another adult, for that matter?

My guess is if you're adding all that up, you're realizing it's not that much time. See, teaching is lonely. You're surrounded by people with whom you have to pretend to be someone else all day. You're not surrounded by your friends, colleagues, or even peers. You're surrounded by kids.

No teacher can do it all on their own. Every teacher is better off when they can work with their colleagues. It's like the expression "iron sharpens iron" (which, my old principal used to say, All. The. Time. It drove me nuts), but it still rings true.

Even if you teach kindergarten, you're still taking your kids out for specials, or electives, or whatever you call them at your school. It's cliché as hell, but it does take a village. And if you're going to survive the school year, you're going to have to get to know the other villagers.

> It does take a village. And if you're going to survive the school year, you're going to have to get to know the other villagers.

How much of a community you have at work will directly impact your ability to get your work done. When questions pile up, problems get messy, or you just need to vent, you're going to need some support to get by.

Being the New Kid on the Block

So, you landed your first teaching gig (you've proven you have the "right stuff"). Or you're a veteran at a new school. However you ended up there, you're new to the building. What happens next will really impact what kind of year you have. Hopefully, you've landed in a very welcoming building where everyone is warm and inviting.

Teacher cliques are very real, sadly. Some established teachers can be surprisingly cold to new teachers. They act like clout at work, or being liked by students, is some type of pie where there are only so many slices to go around. I never subscribed to this mindset; I don't fully get it. You don't have to either, but the reality is, it's real.

First years in a new building can be lonely. Here's what I can tell you: it gets better. As long as you're not actively trying to burn bridges or be offensive, it will get better.

When I moved to a new school after a few years of teaching, I couldn't make headway with this one group of teachers. I wanted to be friends with them, and some were nicer than others, but they just wouldn't let me in, no matter what I did. I would invite them out, visit their classrooms after school, bring them small gifts (like an ice-cold Coke Zero on a hot day), but nothing seemed to work. See, the school experienced a lot of turnover. In any given year, about 30% of the teachers would leave. This group of teachers, who had all been at this school for the last five years, just didn't want to make room for anyone who might not stick around. The following year, 70% of the teachers left, including the "it" group, which gave me my opening.

I made sure to be the friend that I wanted. A new teacher came in mid-year, and I made it a point to befriend them. We are still friends to this day, despite my leaving that school years later and moving 800 miles away. And it got even better after that. Turns out a lot of other teachers didn't love the *Mean Girls* cast and were happy that we got some fresh blood. We formed a bigger circle than ever, were more inclusive, and really turned the school culture around. Sometimes, it's time that's on your side.

Another reason schools with a lot of turnovers can be lonely for new teachers is that the students don't trust that you're actually going to stick around. They will likely call you "teacher" or "mister/miss" for that first year instead of learning your name. But, if you do stick around, it'll be like night and day once the students know you're there for the long haul.

Make your own community if you can't find one. If you're the new kid and no one wants to play ball with you, wait until the new, new kids show up and play ball with them. I assure you, they'll need someone to let them know which things to avoid, how to unjam the copier, and which administrative assistant to go to when you need a favor, and you can be that person for them.

Focus on what you can control and try not to get lost in the drama.

The Work Bestie

Okay, assuming things are going alright for you at your school, you're going to hopefully find a work bestie. Someone who helps you get through the days, weeks, and the time between Spring Break and the end of the school year.

A recent Gallup article emphasizes how important it is to have a best friend at work. Having a best friend at work significantly decreases the likelihood that someone will quit and also improves overall workplace satisfaction (Patel & Plowman, 2024).

The goal here isn't to create a whole clique or club. You just need to find that one person who gets you and whom you can rely on. Maybe it's the person you run into each morning at the copier machine or the other early bird to school (or night owl person staying late getting work done), but you need to find your person.

It doesn't happen overnight, though. According to research by Jeffrey Hall from the University of Kansas, it takes around 200 hours to form a close friendship (Hall, 2018). That is a crapload of time when you're only seeing others for five-minute interactions in the hallway. But it doesn't all have to be time spent at the bar hanging out on Friday (or Wednesday) night. Time at lunch, during your planning period, or even texting during in-service meetings counts. But you will have to put in the time. I've found that it's easiest to make friends with others in a similar situation to yours. If you're new to the school, start with the other new folks. They're probably looking for a connection, too.

How did I find my best work friend? We first bonded over Spirit Week. We were both new teachers to the building, and as young new teachers, we started taking Spirit Week way too seriously. We noticed that each of us was sort of going all out and made a plan to paint our faces for the homecoming game. So we exchanged numbers, bought the paint, and that Friday decked ourselves out in purple and white and went all in, full hype. After that, it was just one thing after another. We became class sponsors together the next year, started sponsoring the same club, going out for Friday drinks, and the rest was history. For the next seven years (before I moved away), he was my ride or die. I had a problem, so I went to him. I couldn't figure something out, so I'd go to him. Someone rubbed him the wrong way in the staff room; he'd come find me on my planning period. You get what I'm saying, we became a dynamic duo that got stuff done. We made each other better, but also made work better.

Two of my other work friends from different schools grew out of carpooling. Gas is expensive and everyone likes not driving sometimes.

At my first job, a new teacher to the school (same situation as me) lived in the apartments across the street from mine. We would carpool every day and that added face time led to a friendship. She still sends me her family's yearly newsletter.

My other buddy from San Jose used to pick me up when my wife and I had only one car. Sure, he was doing all the driving but I would spring for coffee and gas. He was my first friend at the job and my anchor when others weren't being so warm to me.

Another great way to make work friends is to get in a text group. Chances are, teachers at your school already have a text thread. You want to get into the text thread. It will normalize you being included in things, give you the chance to like, love, and "ha-ha" things, and also help you get a feel for who your colleagues are. As Oscar Wilde might've said, "the only thing worse than being in the text group is not being in the text group."

A best friend doesn't just make the job better; it makes it worth sticking around for.

The Ben Franklin Effect

Have you ever heard of the Benjamin Franklin effect? It's this idea that people like us more after doing a small favor for us. So, if you're trying to befriend someone at work, start by asking them for a small favor. Maybe it is to show you something on your learning management system, or to have them send you a slide deck they were using. It doesn't matter what it is, just try not to make it an inconvenience for them. It should be small and doable.

> Not only is asking for help a healthy way to behave, but it also helps us make friends.

Just like we use psychology with our students, we can use it with our peers. So, not only is asking for help a healthy way to behave, but it also helps us make friends.

Common Spaces

Most of the official spaces that exist in a school, in service professional development, staff meetings, etc., are not where the real connections take place. Most connections take place before and after these meetings. That is where you're going to find your people.

The trick is to use these forced interactions to create connections.

Take advantage of the icebreaker questions that we all dread to learn about your coworkers. Remember their names. Their kids' names. Their dog's name. Just remember something. This will give you something to bring up and lean on when you're trying to make friends with them later or start up a chat in the hallway.

These required interactions are also where you can find your people based on views, too. Are you wondering something about the meeting but too afraid to ask? Did someone ask what you wanted? That's your people. Are you bored, and someone just let out an audible sigh at something the meeting leader said? That's your people. Are you eager to be there and trying to take it all in? Look for others sitting on the edge of their seat as well. Take a minute to look around at these things, and you'll learn a lot about who people are. Do this and you're one step closer to building a community.

Lean into unofficial spaces for finding work friends. Hallways, copier queues, and mailboxes, these are all places where people are less likely to be "on" and you're more likely to be able to build a real connection.

Don't Eat Alone

It may be tempting, in fact, it will likely be tempting to eat alone at your desk, trying to catch up on work. I would like to suggest not doing that. Spending time in the lunch room, eating with staff, is a great way to build your community. You don't even have to say much while you're there, but just being there is going to give you a sense of where people stand on issues, who you have things in common with, and possibly who you can go to if you're having issues. The staff lounge is a good place to get those at-bats you need with people. Remember the 200-hour rule? Where else are you going to clock that time?

Not to mention, taking a break for yourself is a good way to help prevent burnout from creeping in. Now, if you're a work-hard, play-hard type and you want to bust it all out while you're at school and leave it all behind when the bell rings, then working through your lunch might be what you need to find peace. But for my money, get to know the teachers who share your lunch.

Toxic Culture

Not all school communities are positive. Sometimes people are cliquey, we've covered this, gossipy, or the worst offenders of all, passive-aggressive. It is more likely than not that you will encounter some combination of these three traits during your time in education. We would like to wish that teachers are better than the students they teach, but sometimes it just isn't that way.

Not every school is a village, and you need to learn to protect your peace. If the staff room is a toxic pit of cynicism and back-biting, avoid it. It sucks, but protect your peace and stop going there. Maybe create a safe haven for others who want to skip the drama, too.

At one school, we had a "no student talk" rule during lunch. We could talk about anything, but not students or the negativity that comes with it. It was a good rule that stopped us from falling into the abyss of constant complaining.

Speaking of that rule, you might need boundaries to keep yourself from being sucked into negativity. I make it very clear that I don't talk poorly about my peers or students, and I shut it down when it comes up. If someone tries to drag you into drama, change the subject politely or be direct: let them know you'd rather keep things positive.

For me, I like to categorize teachers in two ways that help me like everyone. If I can't find a way to like them professionally, then I work to like them personally and vice versa.

It's important to remember, though, that sometimes we're the ones who need a perspective switch. If you find yourself causing problems, gossiping too much, or creating a toxic culture at your school, take a second to reevaluate yourself and maybe check if you're burning out. You can always apologize and do better before it's too late.

Finding Your Community Online

Using the internet is a good way to find community when all else fails, or for just a little extra support. Maybe you're the only teacher at your school in your subject, or even your grade level. In that case, I recommend jumping online to see what is out there.

There is no shortage of Facebook groups for teachers. There are groups for new teachers, ELA teachers, SPED teachers, you name it, there's a group for it. The trick is finding a group that works for you. And that's just on Facebook.

If you do join an online community, remember that you are there for support, and be sure to exit if things turn toxic. If you find yourself comparing your classroom to others or feeling superior, it might be time to log off.

Time Outside the Classroom

Not all relationship building is going to take place during school hours. Many times the best way to get to know people is the time we spend outside of school. Attending social hours and school events are a good way to generate the hours and goodwill needed to make those friends. And remember, I made my best work friend by engaging in homecoming activities.

Be Seen Then Leave

Attending school sporting events, plays, and other things the students involved in are great ways to make friends. You'll run into other teachers there, who will like that you value student activities and you might even get noticed by your administration. However, just because you go to the volleyball game doesn't mean you have to stay until it's over.

Very few people are going to notice whether or not you're there for the buzzer. Show up, high-five enough students to make an impression, give a few shouts, and then make your exit on the way to the bathroom like you're dipping out on a bad first date.

If you're not sure how to pull that off, half-time or intermission is a good time to make your Irish goodbye (leaving without saying anything).

That isn't to say you never stay until the end, but if you follow this advice, you'll boost your clout by being seen and looking involved without having to give up all of your weeknights.

Happy Hours and Social Events

There are other ways to make friends at work too, and some would argue that they are more fun. Work happy hours are a great way to build relationships with staff members. They can quickly turn toxic, so you'll need to be careful, but in general, getting together with your peers will build bridges faster than just hanging out during lunch.

Happy hours are how I met my wife, well, not how I met her, but how we came to be, so of course I view them favorably. If your school doesn't have a happy hour, make your own.

It is important to note that you don't always have to close the bar down when you go out on a Friday after work. In fact, I would argue that nothing good happens after 9 pm at one of these things. People do remember what you say, and if you get too deep in your cups, you run the risk of alienating your peers, which is exactly the opposite of what you want.

The same goes for work parties. At work parties, there is very likely alcohol and people you do not normally go out with. You are more likely to run into someone like we've mentioned earlier, the mean girls, at one of these things. My advice: show up, have a drink, say your hellos, and then say your goodbyes. It is always better to hear about the drama on Monday morning than to be the drama on Friday night.

The Most Important People in the School

The last people we want to talk about here might be the most important for having a great school year. Make friends with the school administrative staff, the custodians, and others who make the school run.

My first year at a school, I brought donuts to the office staff, bought boba tea, and would always bring down any extra snacks I had that students didn't want.

I've also brought in Halloween candy and dropped it off in the custodians' room with a little note. Back when I had a consistent person cleaning my room, I would leave a gift card on my board at Christmas for them as a thank you for taking care of my room.

Needless to say, I never have to wait very long for things I need, and my room is always taken care of.

This might be a little out of your budget, living on first-year teacher wages, but you'd be surprised how far a five-dollar gift card or even a boring old greeting card will get you with people who are commonly overlooked.

Also, the office staff interacts with the administration all the time. If they like you and sing your praises, your bosses are going to hear that too.

Making Inroads

Maybe you don't know anyone well enough to even start to look for a work friend. Maybe you're not sure who you can trust to vent to. Maybe, you're the youngest one on staff or in your department, and people just aren't available to go out on Friday nights (or any night).

Start small. Bring in some donuts or cookies; it doesn't have to be anything crazy, and you don't have to break the bank, but if you show up to the department meeting with a fresh dozen, people are going to remember that.

We Suck Less Together

By this point in this book, you know that teaching is hard. Too hard to do alone. You don't have to be friends with everyone you work with (hell, I even had a frenemy for years at one school), and you don't have to be at every happy hour. You just need a handful of folks to lighten the load. Someone to make you laugh, let you vent, or get your sense of humor.

The truth is, at the risk of sounding cheesy, we do suck less together. It's called a staff, lean on it. When all is said and done, you're going to forget many, if not most, of your students. You will have thousands that walk through your door, but you'll remember the staff that saved you a donut, opened your door when you were running late, or stayed late to set up for homecoming.

So be kind. Be a good teammate. It might start with a favor, it might start with Spirit Week, but if you stay open, you'll find your community—and that's how you suck less together.

Chapter Recap
- Be kind and bring donuts.
- Look out for a work bestie.
- Ask for small favors.
- Use common/unofficial spaces.
- Don't always eat alone.
- Avoid toxic culture.
- Use online communities.
- Attend school events (sports, club fairs, etc.).
- Go to Happy Hour (but don't get messy!).
- Make friends with the staff too.

References

Hall, J. A. (2018). How many hours does it take to make a friend? *Journal of Social and Personal Relationships, 36*(4), 1278–1296. https://doi.org/10.1177/0265407518761225

Patel, D., & Plowman, J. (2024, January 19). Why work friendships matter more than you think. *Gallup.* https://www.gallup.com/workplace/397058/increasing-importance-best-friend-work.aspx

7

Suck Less at Getting Better: Self-Improvement Strategies for a Busy Teacher

Teaching is the hardest job you'll ever love, and getting better at teaching never stops. Whether you're attending a district-mandated PD or simply scrolling through "Teacher Tok," improving at teaching is a daily endeavor. Reading this book is a good first start, but it isn't the end of your journey. Once you get your feet under you, you're going to want to take things to the next level.

The good news is that people have been teaching forever, and there is no shortage of resources out there for you. Thanks to the availability of social media and the internet, it's easier than ever to sharpen your skills.

I know it can feel daunting to think about focusing on the craft of teaching when you're spending so much of your time on the job of teaching. But hopefully, with a little guidance and a little work, we can get you well on your way to making it past the end of the week and beyond.

This chapter is dedicated to what brought me from my rocky beginnings to thriving in the classroom. It's what has worked for me to not only survive but thrive in the classroom.

Watching Others

One of the best ways to improve is to watch others, in real time, work with the same students and population. Most teachers will be fine with having someone come in and observe them, as we, as teachers, are slightly narcissistic (I mean, we did take a job where we are the center of attention) and love to show off—and everyone is used to being observed by administration anyway.

The goal here should be to watch for teacher moves. How do they get the class quiet? Do they have a quiet signal (they should!)? How do they transition or deal with students who are disengaged? What modalities do they use to present information? What tricks or structures can you steal from them? It's okay to steal things. They wouldn't have let you come by if they didn't expect you to take something from their instruction.

What I did when starting at my new school was simply email my department and ask if anyone was okay with me stopping in during my planning period to watch how they teach. Not everyone was game for it, but enough were that I was able to get a feel for how the school operated and what the general expectations were for teachers.

I know, I know. Giving up what precious little time we have in the day can be daunting, and the last thing you want is more work. It's worth it though, watching others will pay dividends down the road. More than any video, book, or PD, learning from watching someone do the job is much more effective. The more you can learn from the teachers who have been in your school longer, the more quickly you can implement what they have figured out. It's like a multiplier effect.

And you don't have to stay for the whole lesson. Ask to observe how they start class—or how they wrap things up, even. You could jump in when they are doing a cool activity or playing a game. Fifteen minutes watching another teacher actually do the thing is going to be more valuable than you can imagine.

Having Others Watch You

Slightly more difficult to arrange, but just as valuable, is having others watch you. Depending on what kind of school you're at, you will be evaluated and observed by your administration, but that comes with so many strings and stresses that it isn't always as fruitful as having a friend or colleague pop in for a lesson (or part of a lesson). Also, I've been at schools where the feedback is on a sticky note with a "Great Job! Keep it Up!" and not really about refining the finer points of my craft. (I've also been at schools where a principal kept track to the minute how much time I spent on each activity).

When having other people come watch you, give them some guidance. It shows you're serious about getting better and respect their time. Let them know, "I'm working on my questioning right now. Can you keep track of what kind of questions I ask my students?" or "My transitions have been taking too long. Do you think you can help me figure out how best to transition?" It could be anything, but frame the observation so you're not getting feedback that is all over the place, or that you're not in the headspace to hear. Sometimes you know you're struggling with a certain student, and you don't need a reminder about it when all you really want is to know if your activity is landing.

Find yourself a critical buddy, though, and see if they can provide you with feedback. If none of your peers are available, usually an instructional coach or department head will make themselves available if asked. The goal here is to be able to focus on improvement and not have the anxiety of whether or not you're getting hired back attached to it.

Watching Yourself

The simplest, and in some ways hardest thing to do, is to watch yourself teach. I have zero doubt that you are in possession of a video recording device in your pocket so if all else fails, set it up at the back of the class, and let it rip.

Watching yourself is the purest, truest way to improve your craft. If you get bored after five minutes of hearing yourself, just imagine what your students are experiencing. Recording your classroom in real time allows you to notice things that you didn't see when you were in the moment. It's kind of like the difference between playing the game and watching the game. When you're under center and there are 300-pound linebackers rushing you, it's not always easy to see the open guy downfield.

I'll be the first to admit that watching yourself can be cringe-inducing, but if you're really stuck in a plateau, it might just be what you need. Taking the outsider's view of watching a video of your class brings clarity or a perspective that you just can't get any other way. So be brave and set up that camera if you're feeling ready.

> Taking the outsider's view of watching a video of your class brings clarity or a perspective that you just can't get any other way.

Mentors and Coaches

Most schools have an instructional coach of some kind. If you're lucky enough to be assigned one, take advantage of it. It doesn't matter if they're old and out of touch or new and green; they're in that role for a reason, and they probably have something you can learn.

Back in Indiana, where I started teaching all new teachers were assigned a mentor. My mentor and I didn't see eye to eye and had different approaches to the classroom. So, when she gave me advice, I ended up ignoring it.

She used to say, "This is how I would do it," and I dismissed her advice. Years later, I realized what she meant was, "This is how I think you should do it." So, if you have a coach or mentor, and they tell you how they'd do it, don't make the same mistake I did. I lost out on the opportunity to really learn from someone who had been doing it because I thought I knew everything I needed to know. Spoiler alert, I didn't. So, do the thing. Don't wait for hindsight to kick in for you to realize you should have taken advantage of the opportunity to grow.

Even the administrators who only spent a few years in the classroom still see things you don't. They're watching your lesson with an outside perspective and comparing it to dozens of other teachers.

It can be hard to hear feedback when someone only watched 15 minutes of your lesson, or came in only at the start, but didn't stick around to see where you were going. But try to be open to what they are saying. You'll thank yourself later down the road.

Using Social Media

Digital resources are a great way to find help on current issues you're having or explore what other teachers are doing outside your school. You may be like I was at my second school, where I was a department of one and had no one to turn to for advice. That's where online resources can help now, with very little lift. So many teachers post tips, tricks, and hacks for the classroom.

TikTok: Get on "Teacher Tok." The algorithm will learn. Just search for teachers and start looking for tips and tricks. I have learned so many things from watching TikTok that I didn't know existed. Be wary, though, as TikTok can quickly become a time suck, and before you know it, you've been online for two hours. I've deleted and reinstalled the app more times than I can count.

YouTube: I learned how to set up and design my canvas page from YouTube. There are so many helpful videos on there, not to mention inspirational TED Talks and other videos to help you keep going when times get rough.

Professional Development

If you're fortunate enough to be at a district that pays to send teachers out to professional development, take advantage of it. If your district will pay to fly you around to learn from the best, apply for every opportunity. In my early years, I was part of a turnaround school and we literally had millions to spend thanks to the School Improvement Grant. I went everywhere.

You might not be in a district with millions to spend on PD, but that doesn't mean you're stuck. Look for something local or drivable, and you'll have a much greater chance of getting it. Online PDs are even more likely to get approved.

The more likely scenario is that you will have in-house PD. Either brought about by the district or an outside contractor who comes and presents to your whole staff. It's likely you already know this, but what I am here to caution you against is adopting the jaded mentality that many of the "old timers" will have. Those of us who have been teaching for a long time have seen trends in education come and go. They have seen district "mandates" get initiated, poorly implemented, and then forgotten. There will be those who simply do not participate in the sessions being presented or undermine them with comments under their breath, or with just apathy. Do not let that happen to you. Even when you are a veteran. Embrace the training. Take what you can from it, even if it's only one thing. Grab something good you can take back to your classroom.

I once attended a conference where I didn't skip any sessions to explore the city, party, or take a long lunch. I was diligent. And every session felt *so boring*. They were mostly teachers presenting about things I already knew, or felt like I already knew.

But, on the very last day, the day that it was just morning sessions, the day that literally everyone else on my team slept in or said they weren't going, I went. I attended a session on summer bridge programs, and it changed my life. I was blown away by what they were doing. The whole conference could have been a bust but I got so much out of that one session, it made the whole thing worth it.

I was able to learn because I was still open, because I didn't skip the conference or just stay at the hotel; I was still looking to learn.

Take what you can from PD. Don't let others around you keep you from learning.

Jugyō Kenkyū

If you're really feeling the itch to get better faster, I recommend the Japanese practice of Jugyō kenkyū, or "lesson study." This requires another teacher to work with in order to pull it off. If you're in a district where the PD just isn't hitting, or doesn't do PD at all, then this might really be something to consider.

Finding others to do this with you will be the hardest part, but if you're able to find someone, it could be the most rewarding growth you've ever experienced.

There are four basic steps to Jugyō kenkyū.

First, you need to collaboratively plan a lesson. That's probably the hardest part, finding time to meet and dealing with different teaching styles. Teachers have a habit of being territorial with their instruction, but if you're able to get past that, it'll be smooth sailing from there. It's important to find someone you connect with for this reason. The more you're able to see each other as peers, the easier it will be to work together. You may recall from this chapter on lesson planning that some of my best lessons were co-planned with other teachers. That's the real value in this. Unlike my planning with a math and special education teacher, Jugyō kenkyū is usually done with teachers of the same subject or grade level.

Second, you teach the lesson while those who helped plan it observe the lesson. Looking for ways to improve the lesson, how did it go? What teacher moves made it stronger? What intangibles existed that made it successful? Then, ideally, your observing teacher would teach it in their class while you observed, looking for the same things.

Next, you meet up again, compare notes, and see what you all saw. This debrief is where self-reflection can happen, and you decide how to improve the lesson for next time.

Lastly, if possible, another teacher would teach the improved lesson, or you could reteach it and see how it goes this time around.

It's a cycle of learning, but one that is worth exploring.

Now, do you have to do this with every lesson you teach? Of course not. But if you have a shared unit in fifth grade coming up, or you're able to find some time with the other IB Global Politics teacher, then give it a whirl. This level of support and scrutiny will improve your instruction in ways that sitting through a PD or reading a book simply cannot.

No Teacher Is an Island

I would not still be teaching today if it weren't for the guidance of other teachers around me. I remember struggling so hard my first year teaching. I went home during winter break and read Harry Wong's *The First Days of School* cover to cover. It had so many things that my teacher course in undergrad just didn't cover.

After that, it was reading *Teaching with Love and Logic*, which helped form the basis for my classroom management approach and quite literally saved my career.

No one can or should go at it alone, and there are so many that have come before us that we can learn from. Below are the books I've found most helpful in my practice, educational or not. After you finish here, check out some of the books below. It is very likely you can find a copy or two of them at your school already stashed away somewhere.

Books That Aren't Mine

I didn't get to where I am today alone. I've studied my craft and the following books are the ones I recommend for continued reading.

Teaching with Love and Logic: This book saved my career. After my utter failure as an eighth-grade teacher, my assistant principal at the time told me to read this book. She was like, "Hey, it's obvious you love your students, but you are not good at classroom management." Or something to that effect.

Anyway, I picked up a copy and was immediately the teacher I always thought I could be. Just kidding. But I did start practicing the things in the book when I was subbing for a semester after leaving my second school. Every day, I would go to work with a new set of students and just practice the moves in this book until they became second nature.

Then I started to finally become the teacher I knew I could be. If you read one book on education this year, read this one. Trust me (Fay & Funk, 1995).

Where Great Teaching Begins: This book is all about writing strong learning objectives. Hence the title.

I ran a book club for this book back when I was an instructional coach because of how good it is. I remember reading this book in year seven of my teaching career, and it made me feel like I didn't know anything about teaching. In a good way. It really blew me away. If you're struggling with assessing learning and planning for learning, check out this book (Reeves, 2011).

Fires in the Bathroom: If you teach at a school with students who are facing more systemic barriers, this book might be one for you.

Written in collaboration with high school students in both Los Angeles and New York City, *Fires in the Bathroom* comes with practical advice for how to navigate these complex relationships (Cushman, 2003).

What Great Teachers Do Differently: This book is a best seller and rightfully so.

In his book, Todd Whitaker shares stories from teachers who are at the top of their game. Each story shares something different they do that we can learn from. It's also on the shorter side, which is nice for a teacher feeling overwhelmed (Whitaker, 2011).

Non-Teaching Books

Not every book that will improve your practice needs to be about teaching. The following few books are ones I found helpful for improving as an educator.

Switch: I mentioned this book earlier. It offers great insight into changing our habits.

If you're struggling with something in the classroom, personally or professionally, this book will help you reassess things and develop habits to make the changes you need (Heath & Heath, 2010).

How Full is Your Bucket?: If you're looking to be inspired a little when it comes to making students happy, this book will definitely be one you will want to read.

How Full is Your Bucket? is rooted in the idea that when we're happy and content, we make those around us happy and content. In my early years, I literally had a checklist on my podium that reminded me to make sure I was filling my students' buckets.

Also, a short read and something you can knock out in a weekend (Rath & Clifton, 2004).

Mindset: I debated about including this book because it is so ubiquitous in education these days. Carol Dweck does a good job of driving home the point of how we need to challenge the fixed mindsets we've been programmed with and embrace a growth mindset. Overall, just good advice for any teacher (Dweck, 2006).

Chapter Recap

Here are things to try:

- Watch others.
- Get watched.
- Watch yourself.
- Lean on mentors/coaches.
- Use social media wisely.
- Take PD seriously.
- Keep learning.

References

Cushman, K. (2003). *Fires in the bathroom: Advice for teachers from high school students.* The New Press.

Dweck, C. S. (2006). *Mindset: The new psychology of success.* Random House.
Fay, J., & Funk, D. (1995). *Teaching with love and logic: Taking control of the classroom.* The Love and Logic Press.
Heath, C., & Heath, D. (2010). *Switch: How to change things when change is hard.* Broadway Books.
Rath, T., & Clifton, D. O. (2004). *How full is your bucket? Positive strategies for work and life.* Gallup Press.
Reeves, A. R. (2011). *Where great teaching begins: Planning for student thinking and learning.* ASCD.
Whitaker, T. (2011). *What great teachers do differently: 17 things that matter most* (2nd ed.). Routledge.

8

Suck Less at Everything Else: Lessons I Wish I'd Known When I Started

Think of this chapter as the "grab bag" chapter of this book. It has some tips and advice that I learned along the way (read: the hard way), or learned from watching others, that didn't really fit anywhere else. It's the stuff I wish someone would have told me or that I would have known when starting out in this career.

As Otto Von Bismarck is credited with saying, "Only a fool learns from his own mistakes. A wise man learns from the mistakes of others." So, I hope this chapter will keep you from making your own mistakes and, hopefully, make teaching just a little easier.

Do Not Reply All

Let's just get this one out there right now. This may or may not be easier depending on the size of the staff at your school, but do not reply to all staff emails. Unless everyone is hopping on a "congratulations" train and you want to add to it, that's fine, but for the sake of all that is holy, do not share your opinions on issues staff-wide. Yes, you may see others doing it. You may even be in the majority opinion. You might even be right. That doesn't matter. Keep it to yourself. Nothing good comes from you sending off a reply all pontificating on a new rule, school-wide initiative, or administrative misstep.

This goes for public Slack, Teams, G-chats, etc. If you put it in writing, anyone can bring it back up later.

Also, your tone cannot carry across text-based messaging, and you run the risk of being misinterpreted. It's better to just avoid it and let the veteran teachers deal with it.

If an issue has you so incensed that you just have to say something, find your mentor, department chair, or trusted ally, and go to them with the issue privately and in person.

Do Not Email Emotionally

You would think this was common sense as well, but you'd be surprised how easy it is to do. It's the end of the day, you've just spent it all with students getting on your last nerves, and an email comes through that just sets you off. Maybe it is something going down that you should have been told about, maybe it's from a parent, most likely it is from someone in a leadership position that forgot to share critical details or made a last-minute change to something important, but regardless, the end result is that it gets under your skin.

You're going to want to reply right away. Who wouldn't? You're fired up, you're pissed off, you've had a day, and now this crap lands in your inbox, come on! Anyway, don't send it. You can type it out and save it as a draft. You can send it to your critical friend, and hopefully you have one by now. You can type it and delete it. There are lots of things you can do, but sending it shouldn't be one of them.

I literally had to put delay on my Gmail that would allow me to unsend or pull back an email after I fired it off. I have gotten much better about this in the years since, but for a while, I was constantly putting my foot in my mouth. Don't be me. Be better.

You Can Be Wrong, Even When You're Right

It was in my fourth-year teaching, and my school had sent a group of us to a conference. We had been shown a video of a couple of teachers running a professional development session. It was not very good. I'm not going to say exactly what I said here, but let's just say I called out, unbeknownst to me, the vice president of the organization. I told him in no short order that his teachers sucked and ours were better. People clapped. The room agreed. But I was the only one to speak up.

Turns out my human resource director was in the room and told the principal to fire me (I was not fired).

After the session was over, several people came up to me and told me I was "right on" or "they were thinking the same thing too," but none of that mattered, because I was the one who took the heat. It didn't matter that I was right. I was marked after that, and for the rest of my time there, I was known as the guy who called out the vice president. I got black listed at my school for years and within the organization.

I wish I could say that was the only time in my career that I pointed out the emperor had no clothes, but it wasn't. I was constantly the guy saying the thing no one else would say. While it did, at times, gain me the admiration of many of my peers, it did not ingratiate me with my administration. Let me be clear, I am not saying to take one for the team to get teachers on your side and speak truth to power. There are times and places for that. But during your first couple of years, until you get established (and ideally tenured), let the leaders be wrong, if it truly matters, they'll figure out their own mistakes eventually or someone more veteran than you will let them know.

This is probably the one thing I wish I learned early on the most. And I have seen many new teachers in schools do this as well, and they might be right, but sometimes that doesn't matter.

"Finsta" Account

Finsta: Noun—a slang term for a fake Instagram account, usually a private one with fewer followers.

In my second year of teaching, I got a Facebook friend request from a member of the school board. I was shocked and a little scared. I was still fresh out of college, and this was the late 2000s, so we were all just posting everything online with little regard to our digital footprint.

Anyway, I was not going to let them see what I had been up to in my undergrad years. So, I created a second account. Turns out to be one of the best things I did. Yes, having a second Facebook is less useful now than it used to be with people abandoning it in favor of Instagram and TikTok, but for years I would add students after they graduated or other teachers, and it became a way to keep in touch without risking my career or embarrassing photos.

My point is, having a fake social media account, or rather a "clean" social media account, might not be the worst idea out there. Make your X or Instagram (or whatever the platform is) private and have one that you can post things about school, your class, or follow the school's account with.

This is a low-level lift that can go a long way.

Extra Clothes

Let me first share what I did, and then I'll get into a story about a friend.

When I taught in New York City, I would commute to work, and it often involved a lot of walking. If you've ever walked a few miles in dress shoes, you know how uncomfortable they can be. So, I started to keep my dress shoes at school and change into sneakers at the end of the day. This way, I was able to be professional, but also comfortable when walking to the subway.

I also used to keep a change of clothes at work for when I would ride my bike. I would change at a local gym nearby where I could shower, but kept the clothes at work so I didn't have to haul them in while riding.

I work with someone right now who has extra shirts in his desk in case he drops food on himself.

This piece of advice might not apply to everyone, but if you hadn't thought of it before, now you have.

Copier Karma

Look, no one wants to be the person to jam the copier. Especially when you're the new person in the building. But don't walk away from a jammed copier. If you jam it, fix it, find someone who can fix it, or tell someone you messed it up. If you jam it and run, people will find out, and you'll look like a jerk.

Also, while we're on it, do not make 3,000 copies in the morning or during lunch. Save that for your planning period or, better yet, after school. One time, a math teacher I worked with made all of her packets for students in the morning, and they were like 25 pages each. No one else could make a copy for hours, literal hours. Packets aren't being used all in one day. If you have a job that large, you'll need to find a time to do it that doesn't block your colleagues. I know as a burned-out, overworked, stressed-out teacher this may be hard and you may feel like you don't have any time to do it but then. If that's the case, I would recommend doing it in chunks so others can jump in if needed. Trust me on this, you won't ingratiate yourself with many if you're always hogging the machine.

If you do make a crap ton of copies, refill the copier with paper. No one has ever complained about someone filling the copier up. In fact, go one step further and put more paper in than you used. Everyone appreciates a fully stocked printer. And, if you made a bunch of copies and someone comes in a hurry to make a quick one, and it's out, oof, that's a bad look too.

Read Your Email

Teachers have a lot going on, and it can be hard to stay up on everything. You don't want to be the only person not ready for a fire drill or something similar because you didn't read your email.

I have a special inbox rule set up so all my emails from administration automatically go to a specific folder for me to check and read. This way, I always know when something important comes in. I also have one for all staff emails, so I know when something a little less important comes in.

Another bad look, especially for a new teacher, is asking questions that were covered in the email. It's okay not to know stuff every now and again, but you don't want to make a habit of not knowing what is going on.

Staff Meetings

This one might sound a bit controversial, especially if you legitimately need to know something but don't ask questions at the end of staff meetings. Everyone is trying to get out of there as quickly as possible. No one likes the person who asks for a point of clarification about something.

Trust me. I know. I was always that guy in the past, even in college. I once worked with a former college classmate who hated me and thought of me as the guy who always made her class run late.

If you're still confused after the meeting is over, read any emails that come out afterwards. Then, if you're still not sure, go to someone you trust and ask them.

Don't Be Seen Behind

I made this mistake in my first year because I remember seeing other teachers do it growing up, but keep your grading in your room. Grading while someone else is watching your students or while someone is trying to teach you something is a big no-no. It doesn't matter how far behind you are in your grading, and no one will care that you haven't slept. Don't grade at meetings.

Additionally, if you're going to call off and grade, stay home to do it. I have known more than one first-year teacher use a day to grade and then sit in the back of their class and do it. This does not make you a martyr to anyone, it just shows how far behind you are. Which, as I've said, is fair and understandable. Grading sucks. But stay home and do it.

Final Thoughts

Teaching isn't just about what goes on in the classroom. It's the little things that make the days and weeks more manageable. The small habits, tips, tricks, or hacks if you will, are what can be the difference between a short stint and a long career.

Every little thing you can do to relieve some of the stress of the job will make a difference. If you can avoid the rookie mistakes and add some preventative measures, you can focus on what really matters: your students.

So don't smash that reply all or email angry, take care of the copier, make sure to check your email, and don't blindside your bosses. You can do it. I believe in you. And if you can't, just keep trying. This is a marathon, not a sprint.

> Every little thing you can do to relieve some of the stress of the job will make a difference.

Chapter Recap

- Don't reply all.
- Don't email angry.
- Don't call out your bosses.
- Keep your private life private.
- You never know when you might need a change of clothes.
- Grade privately.

Epilogue

Suck Less Tomorrow: How It Started, How It's Going

I hope that you have found something in these pages to lighten your load and make your journey a little easier.

This book is the result of hard lessons, misfires, and the kind of failures that only teaching can provide. It's born from a journey of trial, error, and an obsession to get better each day. I've tried to distill what I've learned into something readable, something practical, for you.

As I write this closing chapter, I can't help but think back to when this idea started. It was over 12 years ago when I was an instructional coach (Master Teacher), telling the crop of first-year teachers to "suck less tomorrow." It was working with those green educators that led me to refocus my understanding of what it takes to make it in this job.

We were at a Title 1 school in Northwest Indiana, and it was not an easy teaching environment. The students were challenging, the administration was not as supportive as they could be, and resources were scarce. Needless to say, it was not the place where a teacher could just show up each day and have a rapt audience ready to learn and hang on to their every word.

It was the type of place that teachers would do metaphorical back-flips to keep students engaged and work miracles to reach the diverse levels that existed in their classroom. Every year, we'd burn out someone and they would get replaced by a fresh-out-of-college teacher, a burned-out vet at the end of their career, or someone from Teach For America. It was my job to keep them inspired and improving in the face of all these challenges.

That was how this idea was born. We had PDs, we had copies of *Teach Like a Champion* and *The First Days of School*, but nothing seemed to be landing with teachers. They were grappling every day and just weren't connecting to the resources we had. That was when I started to challenge the champion mindset or the books that don't talk about what to do when things go wrong, and landed on this mantra, "Figure out what went wrong today and commit to try again tomorrow."

My guess is there are things that you are struggling with in the classroom and that's what brought you here. You are finding this job harder than expected because this isn't the job you were promised when you were in school. Colleges and teacher prep programs are woefully underpreparing teachers for the job of teaching, because it isn't a job, it's five jobs. No classroom management course is going to prepare you for when a student is being outright defiant or refusing to even acknowledge your existence, but these things can and do happen.

In college, you were asked to write a handful of lessons; you could take hours to craft them and prepare them, but as you may have learned from student teaching, that kind of time just doesn't exist in the real day-to-day of the job. And that's if you had a teacher prep program. Many teachers today are entering the classroom with little to no actual preparation on how to be a teacher. There are teachers who work for hours when they get home and grade on weekends and appear to have it all together, but that isn't a fair thing to ask of anyone, especially considering what we tend to get paid to do this job.

So, you might be having a hard time at this job but so does everyone else. Everyone, and I mean everyone, every teacher has something they can improve on, some area of weakness or shortcoming, because this is an impossible job to master. I have seen veteran teachers of 20 years fall behind with getting grades in on time. I've seen vets of 30 years struggle to master the school's learning management system, or reply to emails in a timely fashion (or at all). There will likely always be some facet of this job that eludes you because there are so many.

But the point isn't to be perfect. The goal isn't to be flawless at teaching. The goal is to face fewer hurdles in teaching as the years go by. The goal is to survive long enough to turn this into a meaningful and fruitful career you can look back on fondly.

There is no magic bullet lesson plan. In general, in education we are not really sure what works all the time. But we are good at finding things that don't work. So, figure out what isn't working and stop doing that. It's not okay to be complacent with the challenges of teaching. It is okay to be content when facing those challenges because everyone is struggling.

Let me end with a story of a teacher I had in high school for four years. I got to watch my teacher grow up over my time in high school, very much like he got to watch me grow up. I'll be honest, I was not a very good student in high school and this class was no exception, but I did like school and I did like him as a teacher.

I was the second group of students my Japanese teacher, Sparks Sensei ever taught in the United States. He had taught in Japan for three years prior and then moved to the states and began teaching at my school. His first year at my school he had two classes and had to travel 30 minutes down the road to teach two classes at a different school. That first year, when the program started, students had to have a B average to take the class, so he had a sort of head start with that class or at least a group of, for lack of a better word, better students.

Then came year two, when the school opened it up for everyone. That's where I come in. I was not a good student from the get-go and never really studied much. I'm part Japanese, so I had a little intrinsic motivation to learn, but mostly I just hung out with my friends in that class.

I remember year two (so three for my teacher), our class was talking so much that he just got up and left the room. He told us to figure out what we were doing, and he would be back when we were ready to learn. We had literally pushed him to their limit.

But then something started to change. It was my senior year and I was talking to a second-year Japanese student, they were learning what we had learned as fourth-year students. I realized that Sparks Sensei was moving faster through the curriculum and that the lower classes were learning more than we were.

I was not shocked or angry, but impressed. It clicked for me that he was getting better. He was improving on his classroom management, obviously, or he couldn't get through the content, but he was getting better at lesson planning, curriculum mapping, lesson delivery, and expectations. A few years after I graduated, his students went on to win the National Japan Bowl for three out of four years and have won the state level competition 23 freaking times. That means, two years after I graduated (yeah, you can do the math now), they started winning titles.

Did this improvement happen overnight or in a vacuum? Not at all. What happened was that when he was hired by the two schools, he had no formal training in education. He could speak Japanese, so was given the job, but outside of time teaching English in Japan to elementary students, his teacher prep was non-existent.

What happened was he started putting in the work. He enrolled in course to get his teacher training and started working to be a better teacher. One thing he truly credits to his development was the teachers he met and learned from by attending the state's foreign language teacher conference. Those connections helped him survive and thrive. Or to quote him, "I wouldn't have survived without those connections and everything I learned at the conferences."

This is what it means to suck less tomorrow. Did my Japanese teacher struggle in his first year with us? Undoubtedly. He was figuring out how to teach in the states, deal with us knuckleheads, and find what was important to teach. But by year seven and eight, he was getting dialed in. He had started to get his footing, and you can only get there by figuring out what isn't working. By scrapping things that went poorly, by being committed to improving tomorrow to be better than you were today.

I think about my Japanese teacher a lot when thinking about education. I think that his story is just how are in education. Your first-year students will not learn as much as your second year, or your third year, or fourth, etc., etc., etc. That's the way it goes, and that is the way it has always gone. "Naturals" might exist, but for most of us, it's a long game of incremental improvement.

So that's it. That's the basis for my pedagogical philosophy. One teacher's journey that I have seen played out over and over again. Through all my years and teaching across the country this is what I have come to realize. There is no shortcut to great teaching. There's no magic bullet for great teaching. It's like eating an elephant, one bite at a time. But if you keep working, you'll get there.

So, don't kill yourself trying to be the teacher you will be in 20 years in your first years. Just be the best teacher you can be today. If you can do that, if you can focus on gradual improvement, then you'll be able to suck less tomorrow, and *that's* how great teachers are made.

Appendix
Field-Tested Strategies

Well, you made it to the end of this book. Congratulations. There are no medals, but you're reading the appendix, so I did something right, and you must have learned something too.

What I have prepared for you here is a collection of teaching strategies that can be popped into any lesson and create effective learning. It's a way of taking the cognitive load off your shoulders and replacing it with some tried-and-true exercises.

If you rotate around the strategies below, your lessons won't be stale, and students won't get too bored doing the same thing every day.

For each of these strategies, be sure to model them the first couple of times you use them until your students become familiar with them and can do them with less prompting or direction.

I've listed them in alphabetical order, not the order in which I think they are more or less effective or useful.

The strategies included are:

- Class Bingo
- Fishbowl
- Frayer Model
- Gallery Walk
- Jigsaw
- List, Label, Group
- R.A.F.T. and G.R.A.S.P.S.
- Say Something and Sentence Stems
- Snowball Quiz
- Socratic Seminar
- Think-Pair-Share
- Turn and Talk.

Class Bingo

What It Is
This one's pretty straightforward, but I'll explain it anyway—and give a few ideas for how I use it in my classroom.

Class Bingo is basically a classroom scavenger hunt disguised as a game. Will students see through it? Maybe, but if it gets them up and moving, it's a win as far as I'm concerned.

What you do is create a bingo card with 25 prompts, and students go around the room talking to their classmates to fill it out. The first student to declare "Bingo!" gets a prize (stickers, candy, a high five—you decide).

How to Use It
Icebreaker/Class Building
Use it during the first week of school to get students up, moving, and talking to one another. Fill the bingo card with prompts like:

- "Takes the bus to school"
- "Has a pet"
- "Can speak another language"
- "Was born in a different state."

This helps students learn about each other, learn some names, and maybe run out the clock a little. If you're wondering whether students knowing each other's names and interests actually helps the year, go better, it does. The more connected they are, the easier group work, partner tasks, and classroom culture will be later.

Review Game
You can also use Class Bingo as a content review.

- Fill the squares with vocabulary terms and have students find classmates who can define them.
- Or images (say, of historical figures or literary symbols), and students find someone who can ID each one.
- Or facts, dates, formulas—whatever you've been teaching.

The format is flexible. It's quick to set up, gets them talking, and works for both academic review and social bonding. The best part is that it can fit in any lesson when you have 15–20 minutes to burn.

After students are done and someone has won, you can then review the squares with the class as a further extension activity.

Fishbowl

What It Is
Fishbowl is a discussion technique where a small group of students sits in the middle of the room and actively discusses a topic, while the rest of the class sits around them as listeners. The students in the center engage deeply, and those on the outside observe, take notes, or reflect.

How to Use It

- **After a Reading:** Select a few students to discuss the material while others listen and take notes.
- **Expert Groups:** Assign small groups to study a section of a text or topic in detail. Each group discusses its part in the fishbowl while the rest listen. Rotate groups to give everyone a chance.
- **Hot Topics:** Use a small, articulate group to navigate sensitive or divisive discussions, instead of just a free-for-all, large group conversation.
- **Pro/Con Conversations:** Instead of a whole-class debate, have a small group split into opposing sides to discuss the issue, providing focused and balanced perspectives.

Frayer Model

What It Is
The Frayer Model is a graphic organizer developed by Dorothy Frayer in 1969 at the University of Wisconsin (Frayer, Frederick, &

Klausmeier, 1969). It's a way for students to learn new concepts or vocabulary words.

The graphic organizer puts the new word or concept in the middle of the page and then has students use the rest of the paper to do a variety of things, as there are variations on the theme here, depending on the teacher.

Common categories I have seen are definition, picture, characteristics, examples, non-examples, and use it in a sentence. There are many different ways to use it.

While I do use the Frayer Model in my classroom, I use it sparingly or as a group activity. I've seen teachers think they need to use this for every new word or concept, and students end up making ten of these in one class. Don't do that. Pick one or maybe two high-leverage words and concepts and have students do it that way.

When I said I use it as a group thing, I use it like a jigsaw. Each member of the group has a word, they do the model, and then share their Frayer Model with their group members. This way, everyone benefits from cognitive thinking.

How to Use It

- New concepts in class (such as photosynthesis or irrational numbers)
- New terms or definitions
- Abstract ideals
- Central themes or ideas.

Example Frayer Model

Gallery Walk

What It Is

A gallery walk gets students out of their seats and moving around the room. Here you'll hang pictures or sentences around

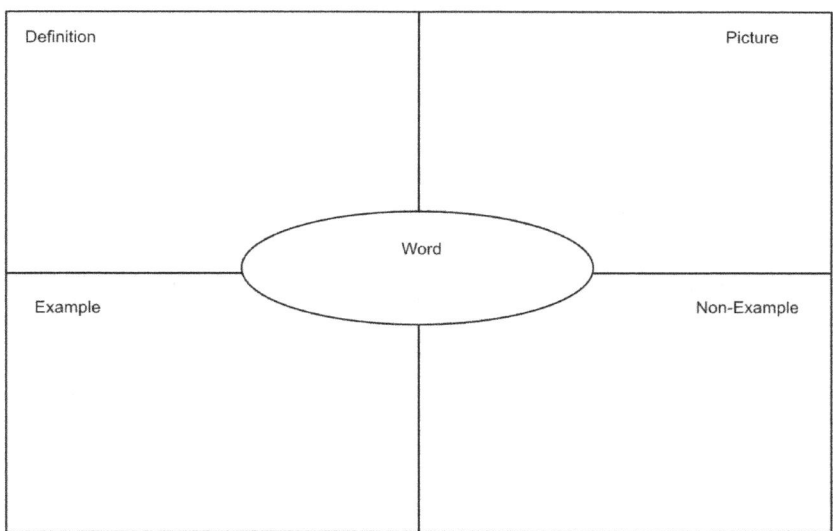

FIGURE A.1 Sample Frayer Model

the room, and students will move around the room and review them all.

This is another good way to get students up and moving, which also helps with classroom management.

How to Use It

1. **Introducing a new topic**—Have students review pictures, vocabulary, or sentence stems for a new topic or unit. This will activate prior knowledge or prime them with information before the lesson begins.
2. **Reviewing a topic**—Students can review previously learned concepts while walking around the room.
3. **Voting**—Students walk around the room with stars, stickers, and/or markers and use them to "vote" or show how they feel about what is being displayed. This can be used when what is being shown in the gallery walk is student work.

Jigsaw

What It Is

Originally developed by social psychologist Elliot Aronson to break down systemic barriers between social groups, the jigsaw is a useful tool for disseminating information and getting students to talk to each other (Aronson, 1978).

A jigsaw is a strategy for dispensing a large amount of information all at the same time to your students. What you do is split the information up into different stations or chunks and distribute those to groups of students who will then become the "experts" of that information.

These expert groups will then convene to share what they have learned about the topic with their home group. This way, each member of the group is dependent on the other members of the group in order to be successful.

How to Use It

- **Content Specific**: In science, students could learn about various biomes, in social studies, they might learn about different Civil Rights movements, and in ELA, they could learn about different characters from a novel.
- **Steps for Completion**: Each group could learn about one step of a longer process, such as a project or lab, and then report back on what the step will be.
- **Breaking Up Chapters**: Each expert would read about one section from the book and then report back on what they learned.
- **Vocabulary**: Students could learn new, unfamiliar words and bring those definitions back, maybe after completing a word diagram or Frayer Model.

Long story short, the jigsaw is a very versatile and useful strategy for introducing new content, especially when students just need to get the gist of something, and it won't be too heavily tested. That's a pro-tip right there. Don't quiz students about information from a jigsaw unless you've given them some kind of guide, because not every expert group will be as thorough.

List, Label, Group

What It Is
List, label, group is a pre-work or pre-reading strategy that can also be a post-work or closing activity when revisited.

Students will be given a list of terms and asked to sort them into groups. Oftentimes, this is facilitated with sticky notes or whiteboards, but the students are told to group them however they feel.

This will force students to draw connections between the words, looking for similarities and differences as they sort the words into different groups.

So, the students are given a list of words, they then group them, and then label the group. I suppose it should be called list, group, label, but that doesn't really roll off the tongue now, does it?

Let's take this list of words to demonstrate how students might do this. This is a pretty basic list of words, and you might want things more content-specific, like abiotic or constitutional, but for the sake of this exercise, we're using these words.

- Apple
- Dog
- Basketball
- Book
- Hammer
- Carrot
- Firefighter
- Pencil
- Ocean
- Sun.

Possible Groups:

- Things you find in a school, kitchen, and universe
- Round vs. Not Round
- Living vs. Not Living
- Natural vs. Man-Made.

How to Use It

- As a pre-reading activity, before a chapter, give students a list of unfamiliar words.
- As a post-reading, students revisit their groups after learning the words to make changes.
- To prime students to be familiar with words.
- As a team-building exercise or class builder, like in the game "soup, salad, sandwich."

R.A.F.T. and/or G.R.A.S.P.S. Writing

What It Is

I've grouped these two together because they are similar in context. R.A.F.T. writing was developed by Doug Buehl (Buehl, 2001), and G.R.A.S.P.S. is found in *Understanding by Design,* by Grant Wiggins and Jay McTighe (Wiggins & McTighe, 2005).

What both of these writing practices do is have students take on a role and create a product.

R.A.F.T. stands for "Role, Audience, Format, Topic," and G.R.A.S.P.S. is "Goal, Role, Audience, Situation, Product/Performance, Standards."

Both are useful when having students summarize or close a lesson. The level of how detailed you want to be will determine which one you might use. My advice is to pick the one that works for your class and then stick with it, so your students will be familiar.

Example R.A.F.T.:

Role: Electron—Students are writing from the perspective of an electron.
Audience: Proton—Their message is directed to a proton.
Format: Sonnet—Students are writing a poem.
Topic: Ionic bonding—The poem should include elements of ionic bonding.

Example G.R.A.S.P.S.:

Goal: Persuade American colonists to fight against England.
Role: Political activist in Boston in 1775.
Audience: Other colonists in Boston or the surrounding areas.
Situation: High tensions after the passing of the Intolerable Acts and the Boston Massacre.
Product/Performance: Create a flyer or brochure to persuade colonists.
Standards: Include three grievances, use persuasive language, contain a call to action, and demonstrate historical accuracy.

Using these examples, you can see how similar and different they are, but both essentially ask students to do the same thing. You might also consider the level of your students when considering which format to use.

How to Use It

- After direct instruction to increase the "stickiness" of the material.
- End of unit of instruction as a summative assignment.
- As part of a Wrap-Up for students to close a lesson.
- As a formative assessment.
- As a differentiation tool based on students' readiness. (e.g., poems will vary, brochures will be of different detail levels, etc., but all students can be successful with these tasks).

Say Something and Sentence Stems

What It Is

Say Something is a reading strategy that can be done in whole group class reading, group reading, or partner reading. It can also be used after an independent reading.

This structure is designed to help students engage with the text by "saying something" about what they are reading. It can be a comment, a prediction, a question, or a connection. As long as it relates back to the text. I used this practice extensively when I taught middle school, and even when I taught lower high school grades.

Say Something was developed by Kylene Beers, a renowned literacy expert, and popularized in her book: *When Kids Can't Read—What Teachers Can Do* (Beers, 2003).

For setup, have sentence stems ready for students to use. I would print them out and have them on their desks. Back when I kept binders for each group, I would have a copy of them permanently with them to refer back to.

Examples of stems are:

- I predict that...
- I wonder...
- This reminds me of...
- I'm confused about...
- I noticed...
- This is important because...

An internet search will return premade cards from various sources that you can use.

To use this effectively, you should chunk your text before students read, so they will know when they will be prompted to say something. If doing a partner read, each reading partner will be able to use the protocol following their reading. If doing a whole class reading, you could take volunteers, have a student read a comment, or cold call students to respond.

What is nice about having the stems is that it makes cold calling a little less intimidating, as they just need to complete the sentence with what was read.

Having sentence stems around in the classroom is a great way to help guide conversations and can have multiple applications outside of this specific structure.

How to Use It

- Following a whole-class reading.
- While watching a video, pause and ask students to "say something" about the clip they watched.

- During direct instruction, pause after key information and allow students to answer.
- While doing group or partner reading.
- When responding during a fishbowl or Socratic seminar.

Snowball Quiz

What It Is
This is a Wrap-Up strategy that I enjoy because it forces students to get out of their comfort zone. This strategy is widely used, and it was my first-year students who told me about it because their seventh-grade teacher did it. It's wasteful, sure, but a good time if you have a class that can handle it. It can also show that you can let your hair down, so to speak, which is great for students to see.

Anyway, this can be used at any point during a lesson when things are dragging, or you need to do a check for understanding.

How to Set It Up
For this, have students take out a sheet of paper and write a question on it, one that they know the answer to. It should go without saying, but the question should be related to your instruction (though you could use this as an ice breaker if you wanted). Make sure students put their name on the paper so whoever finds the paper can check their answer.

After all the questions are written, you have students crumble the paper into balls. This is a lot of fun the first time you do it because students are usually freaked out by being told to crumble up their questions.

Now the fun begins, you set a time limit and have students start throwing the balls around the room and at each other (be aware of your students who may be unable to handle this, either behaviorally or emotionally). After the chaos has subsided, have students pick up the ball closest to them, unroll it, and answer the question. Next, students will find the person who wrote the question and check to see if they answered correctly.

Note: You may want to guide students in what kind of questions they ask, such as multiple choice, true or false, open-ended, etc.

Steps

1. Write the question and name on paper. (Use scrap paper if possible.)
2. Crumble paper into balls.
3. Toss balls around the room. (For classes that need more structure, you could do this in volleys, such as throw, pick up; repeat until the balls are mixed up.)
4. Find a ball close to you.
5. Answer the question.
6. Check the answer.

How to Use It

- To break up instruction and check for understanding.
- At the end of a lesson.
- Following a large block of instruction.
- After reading a passage or text.
- Following a video.

Socratic Seminar

What It Is

Socratic Seminar is a collaborative, student-led conversation that encourages critical thinking, active listening, and respectful dialogue. It's less about "right answers" and more about exploring concepts and deepening understanding.

Following a reading, a movie, or something that students explore on their own or as a class, you bring the students together to discuss the content, usually with a prompt or starting question.

The success of your seminars will vary based on your grade level and student engagement. But you can run a seminar in elementary classes following a story with a strong moral lesson, for example, or do one in an IB Theory of Knowledge class discussing the merits of a think piece. There are endless possibilities for a good seminar.

The hardest part, for me, is not jumping in when students aren't talking. It's hard to let the class fall silent, but sometimes that happens while students gather their nerve to speak, or check their notes. If you can, fight the urge to jump in and guide them and let them do the heavy lifting.

You'll want to lay some ground rules for your students as well. Some examples I've used and seen are about being respectful, grounding your claims in evidence, and summarizing what you heard before commenting.

How to Set It Up

There are different models for this that you can use. I'll briefly describe what some do and then, in more detail, share what works for me.

I know teachers who take their classes to the lecture hall and have whole-class discussions. For me, this is difficult to get everyone involved, and another instance where we can get "hogs and logs," or those who want to overshare and those who will hide and say nothing.

Some teachers put their desks in a giant circle and have the class face each other and discuss the topic. This is a little more intimate but, for my money, leads to the same issues as above.

Keeping track of who is speaking can also be a challenge for teachers running the seminar. I have written names on the board as they go, kept a notebook, printed out a roster beforehand, and put checks next to names. Any one of these works, but puts the onus on the teacher for keeping track of things.

After many years of less-than-ideal Socratic Seminars, I have landed upon a model that I believe is most effective. Other teachers I know have also adopted this model in their classrooms, so there is a little more field-testing of this strategy.

The first step is to divide your class into two even groups. If you have a group of three, that's fine if it has to happen, but the goal here is to have partners.

Next, you're going to turn your classroom into a fishbowl discussion (see above) where one half of the class will be discussing the seminar while the other group is actively listening.

Here is where things change up from above even more.

The listening partner has what I have created as the "Socrative scorecard," where they are keeping track of what their partner is saying, points they made, opinions vs. facts they share, and then providing a summary and feedback to their partner. They aren't just sitting idly by doing nothing.

I've also added two-color chips for students to keep in front of them while in the fishbowl. Each student gets three and must flip each over to earn full credit for the discussion, but is also limited to three shares, until everyone has shared three times. The chips help to alleviate the "hogs and logs" dilemma by encouraging participation and more thoughtfulness over what to share.

I generally set a timer for the seminar as well, so students know how long they have to get their points and create a sense of urgency to keep things moving.

You can download a free copy of the Socratic Seminar from www.wesucklesstomorrow.com under resources. Feel free to copy or build your own based on my model below.

How to Use It

- Following a reading (article, book, think piece, something with some heft).
- After a video clip or movie.
- After a unit of instruction (Civil War, Evolution, etc.)
- Anytime students might have differing views or internal confusion about an issue (I realize that isn't super helpful, but you'll probably be able to identify when it is a good time for a Socratic Seminar).

Name:	Partner Name:
☐ Partner spoke at least 3 times ☐ Partner referred to the text or material at least once ☐ Partner asked a question OR responded directly to a peer ☐ Partner distinguished between opinion and evidence ☐ Partner built on someone else's idea ☐ Partner listened respectfully (e.g., didn't interrupt)	Key Idea Shared:
Facts Referenced:	Opinions Shared:
Text referenced:	Questions Asked:
Feedback for partner:	

FIGURE A.2 Socratic Score Card

Think-Pair-Share

What It Is

Think-Pair-Share is a discussion strategy that encourages students to think about a concept or idea and then share it with a partner. It's a low-prep activity that requires very little setup.

First, have students think about a prompt. It could be "What is the central conflict in this story?" for example. I like to have students write their answers down so they are committing to their thinking and don't change it after hearing their partner share.

Next, students share with a partner. Most teachers have students turn and talk to someone next to them, but you could also do a mixing activity or some other strategy that has them find a friend across the room.

Lastly, of course, they share what they thought or wrote down with their partner.

When I do these activities, I like to call on students and ask them what their partner said. I try to get them to share what they heard, to encourage listening, but also recall. After a few of the cold calls of "tell me what you heard," I'll allow a few students to share what they thought.

The nice thing about this structure is that it is quick and gives students time to process, which is key to learning. Because of its quick nature and setup, you can do it multiple times per class period.

> Pro-Tip: Build this into your slide deck if you're using one. Have it built in so you don't skip, and it gives you time to think out your questions in advance.

How to Use It

- Anytime you need a break in instruction, such as after a chunk of notes or direct instruction.
- Following a short video or clip.
- Before, during, or after a reading.
- Use it as a Warm-Up to get students moving or a Wrap-Up to close a lesson.

Turn and Talks

If you thought Think-Pair-Share was low prep, then strap in, buckaroo.

It is very likely you have experienced this already in high school, college, or maybe a PD, but I'll throw it in here because, believe it or not, some teachers need it. If you're already familiar with this strategy, you can stop reading here. Congratulations: you've finished this book!

For the rest of you, Turn and Talk is exactly what it sounds like. You ask your students to turn and talk to a partner who is sitting next to them.

What It Is

It is often unstructured, with who is doing the speaking, which can be a problem, but usually you're just trying to get students talking and aren't really keeping points for accountability.

Set a timer, or pretend to set a timer, for the talking. It'll sound like "For 2 minutes, turn and talk to your neighbor about the reasons for US involvement in the Vietnam War."

Then you let them talk, of course, while walking around the room pretending to listen in on all the conversations. I kid, but obviously, with everyone talking, you can't track them all.

Anyway, I wrap this up the same way I do Think-Pair-Share. I call on students and ask them what they heard. If the time wasn't enough for both partners to share, I'll ask them what they said.

Since there isn't the pre-thinking and writing activity leading into this, I'm less strict about having everyone share. Though that is the goal, but again, hogs and logs.

Common Pitfalls

- ◆ One student dominates the conversation.
  - Set some guidelines or gentle reminders about being a good partner.
  - Decide who will go first when sharing.
- ◆ Students get off task and talk about something else.
  - Rotate around the room, checking in with students.
  - Let them see you listening.
  - Call on the students not following directions a few times, they'll get it. (There is a fine line between

embarrassing students and holding them accountable. Be sure to be on the latter side of things.)
- Shy students don't participate.
  - Decide who will go first. Putting them on the spot to go first will increase the participation.
- Too much or too little time.
  - It's better to err on the side of too little and leave them wanting more.
  - Experiment with different times, but generally one to two minutes is ideal.
- Students are rushing through without really thinking about the prompt.
  - Encourage students to reference the text or learning when sharing.
- The teacher moves ahead without referencing the Turn and Talk, thus making it seem unimportant to students.
  - Practice, practice, practice.
  - Bring it back to the whole group. Clarify misunderstandings. All things get better with time.

How to Use It

- Breaking up direct instruction.
- After reading a chunk of text (I wouldn't use it for a full review; I would do something more robust for that).
- After a short video clip.
- Following a Warm-Up question.
- After learning new steps to a problem (such as "turn and talk to a neighbor and explain how to find the area of a triangle").

These strategies are tools for your toolbox. Many of us went to school with teachers who just did the same old "lecture, textbook, worksheet, repeat," and that is what we think teaching *is*. As we covered in Chapter 2, students benefit from different modalities and variation.

Rotate around these strategies, mix and match them throughout your lessons. Hopefully, they'll stretch you just enough to help you grow and make you a more dynamic and effective teacher!

References

Aronson, E. (1978). *The jigsaw classroom*. Sage.

Beers, K. (2003). *When kids can't read: What teachers can do*. Heinemann.

Buehl, D. (2001). *Classroom strategies for interactive learning*. International Reading Association.

Frayer, D. A., Frederick, W. C., & Klausmeier, H. J. (1969). *A schema for testing the level of cognitive mastery*. Wisconsin Center for Education Research.

Wiggins, G., & McTighe, J. (2005). *Understanding by design* (Expanded 2nd ed.). Association for Supervision and Curriculum Development.

For Product Safety Concerns and Information please contact our EU representative GPSR@taylorandfrancis.com
Taylor & Francis Verlag GmbH, Kaufingerstraße 24, 80331 München, Germany

www.ingramcontent.com/pod-product-compliance
Lightning Source LLC
Chambersburg PA
CBHW061450300426
44114CB00014B/1913